Meditation
and the creative imperative

COMPASS OF MIND

Knowledge is a dangerous thing, as Adam and Eve found out in the Garden of Eden. Yet without it, humanity would not evolve. Knowledge leads to new pathways of understanding, shaping our views of the world and extending our ability to create. Sometimes ways in which to apply knowledge are sought; at others, knowledge itself is enough, for it is said that man is made in the image of God, and, through knowing himself, can know the divine.

The series 'Compass of Mind' is founded in this view of an integrated physical, human and spiritual universe. It looks at various ways in which knowledge is discovered and formulated, drawing themes from mystical and esoteric traditions, from the creative arts, and from therapies and broad-based science. For each topic the questions are posed: 'What kind of a map of the world is this?' and 'What special insights does it bring?' The series title embodies the concept that knowledge begins and ends with mind; a question asked expands into a circle which is both defined and investigated by mind itself.

Authors of 'Compass of Mind' titles bring a wide perspective and a depth of personal experience to their chosen themes. Each text is written with clarity and sympathy, attractive to the lay reader and specialist alike. Themes are illustrated with lively, well-researched examples, aimed at revealing the essence of the subject, for these are books which tackle the question of 'Why?' rather than 'How to?'

Cherry Gilchrist, series editor

MEDITATION

and the creative imperative

LUCY OLIVER

DRYAD PRESS LIMITED
LONDON

*Dedicated to that unbroken tradition sometimes known as
the Brothers and Sisters of the Common Life*

© Lucy Oliver 1987
First published 1987
Typeset by
Progress Filmsetting Limited,
79 Leonard Street, London EC2
Printed by Biddles Ltd,
Guildford, Surrey
for the publishers
Dryad Press Limited,
8 Cavendish Square,
London W1M 0AJ

ISBN 0 8521 9698 9

CONTENTS

Acknowledgment
The cover illustration is by Gila Zur.

Introduction

The Essence of Meditation

The purpose of this book is to look into the principles of the activity which is called meditation. It is not a survey and comparison of different approaches to meditation, nor does it expound the practices and goals of a particular tradition. Neither is it a self-tutor describing techniques to be followed. It is a study of the process which is initiated when someone seriously begins to meditate in any tradition, or with any technique, and the aim is to make meditation more comprehensible and to widen perspectives. The book is intended as a guide, and one to which a person practising meditation of any kind can return over the years as his or her meditation deepens.

Meditation is as old as humanity. It may be called by other names, but it is a strand which has its origins in the beginning of human consciousness. When you understand meditation, you become aware of the reality of the link between yourself and other meditators, both in the present and reaching back into the past. This is the lineage of meditation. This book draws upon this lineage, and upon the knowledge and skills which form the basis of all traditions.

Meditation is as natural as any other human activity. Human beings can lead perfectly normal, reasonable lives utilizing only a fraction of the potential for awareness which is our birthright as Homo Sapiens. In essence, meditation is a method for increasing awareness and, with it, creativity and the ability to see meaning in life.

In perhaps everyone, questions surface from time to time: What is life for? Where do we come from, where do we go, and why? What is the purpose of existence? Such questioning, unique, on this earth, to humanity, arises because we are self-aware beings. There is also an intuitive recognition that answers are possible, and what is more, that they can be within the experience of an individual human being. Many philosophies, religions and mythologies have formulated the answers in different ways, but the formulations are not the answers. Each individual can re-discover for him or herself the reality which underlies these formulations, and is able to do so because within each individual there is the potential for absolute knowledge of humanity.

Meditation is a process for unlocking this knowledge, for making it conscious. It is best described as an unfolding, as a flower unfolds from a tight little bud, or as a tree develops from a tiny seed. It is growth, but not in the sense of simply enlarging. Cut open a seed, and you do not find a miniature tree. Where is the organization for the massive structure of trunk, branch and leaf? It is encoded in the seed, in potential, awaiting the conditions which will allow it to unfold and grow. Much of the potential of human-ness remains in seed form. Some of the seeds unfold in the conditions provided by normal development to adulthood. The rest await further conditions.

The underlying unity of human beings is that all our bodies and psyches are constructed on the same principles. The manifest diversity of physical and psychological characteristics arises from the ordering and combination of these fundamental principles. Because meditation is a process, not a matter of ideas, beliefs or feelings, it pierces through diversity and works with the roots of being, with that which is common to human beings of whatever racial, cultural or religious background. Meditation triggers the unfolding of what may otherwise remain in potential. The knowledge of meditation has been systematized and passed down within the major meditational traditions, Eastern and Western.

These different meditation systems describe the goals and effects of meditation in the terminologies of the culture or religion from which they have arisen, almost as if they are dealing with different realities. Of course that cannot be so. It is the description which varies, the choice of words and images to describe a *human* process which cannot do other than follow a similar pattern in a human being from east, west, north or south.

Perplexity in face of this diversity of description should not obscure the single essence of meditation, which is the unfolding of the potential of being human. Related to this potential, and part of the mystery of being human, is that which from the beginning of human history has been called divine. It is at the heart, or root, of the process.

Distilling the Essence

The intention throughout the book is not to expound yet another set of descriptions, but to encourage *first-hand* experience and exploration and to present material to assist this. Even the profounder goals of the meditative process can be expressed in terms which are simple and clear. These goals can be identified by a person of any cultural or religious background who is able to stand back enough to distinguish the *nature* of an experience from the particular *form* in which it occurred to him or her. With actual experience of the deeper reaches of being human, the problem of warring ideologies and of belief systems which seem to contradict each other disappears.

There is a great deal of superstition and unnecessary complication about the methods and consequences of meditation. Enormous elaborations and mystifications have inevitably evolved in its long history, often obscuring the essence of the process, and the essential simplicity behind the techniques. It can be both confusing and daunting or entrap you in a web of ideas and theory, which actually forms a barrier to direct experience.

There is a degree of variety in the way meditation can be approached, and exactly what techniques are used. The intention of this book is to take all valid techniques back to first principles, to clarify their operations, and to discuss their consequences for the whole of a person's nature and life. States of consciousness, altered or otherwise, do not belong only in a Psychological Laboratory, or in a monastery or ashram. We all begin in the same place and work with the same materials. We may choose a more specialized environment to undertake the work of meditation, or we may conduct the same work just as successfully in a busy urban lifestyle, though the approach must then be tailored to ordinary life.

Meditation as a Journey

Meditation is a demanding activity. It demands trust, persistence, self-discipline and courage, but the rewards are incalculable. What meditation does *not* demand is a crystalline conception of the aiming point. To begin meditating from some not very clearly defined feeling that it is 'a good thing to do', or from a need to bring some calm or space into one's life, or to be rid of unnecessary tension, is fine. To begin from a desire to become one with the divine is also fine.

Meditation is like undertaking a journey into realms of one's own potential which otherwise remain undiscovered. It is a journey of depth, progressive in that once begun, for whatever reason, new possibilities continually open up if one wishes to take them. Provided it is under competent instruction, the process of meditating will itself present and expand possibilities, and one's goals and perspectives may alter.

As it is intended as a sort of manual for travellers, the book reflects this journey. The earlier chapters outline the principles involved in acquiring the skill of meditation and should continue to be useful at any stage of meditation. The later chapters should expand in meaning with time, as the meditator's understanding and experience deepen.

The metaphor of a journey is misleading, however, if it gives the impression of somehow 'going out' from oneself and one's ordinary life; of ending up 'somewhere else', as another, far better person. The journey is a voyage of discovery which can begin right in the middle of the daily chores, in office, home, bedsit, factory, and it will not alter the need for these mundane realities. It will change them gradually, giving them more meaning, by transforming the weary, bored, trapped or frustrated doer into a person with purpose, energy and abilities he or she had never suspected were present. In other words, at the end of the journey you are where you started, as none other than yourself, yet paradoxically, all is changed.

Human Structure

As well as tracing the stages of a journey, the sections of the book also reflect human structure. Each human being creates around him or herself a world in which to live. It is the product of countless choices of direction and preferences right from the beginning of life, a creation which is, in essence, a working organization in each of the three aspects which characterize human functioning.

In the first place we are *physical* beings, unavoidably operating through a body with its own habits, its particular strengths and weaknesses, its needs, its capabilities. We are also *emotional* beings, our energy levels rising and falling in response to emotional factors and stimuli. We need both emotional input and ways of expressing emotion, and, whether we realize it or not, feelings actually dictate a large proportion of both action and values. A third distinct functional mode is *thought*. We are able to think things through, to perceive logic and consequences. We each need some sort of conceptual structure to make sense of experience, and to order the personal universe in which we live.

The physical organization 'sets', as it were, when the body is fully grown and at the peak of its capacities. By and large it will not change structurally any more. Emotional organization is usually completed in young adulthood, and conceptual organization established generally not long after. From then, both these types of basic psychological settings also change only in detail, not in structure.

Once they are set, inertia usually dictates that all new experience is logged and assimilated according to a person's individual organization. The organization may absorb more information, may extend its limits or increase in variety, but the actual principles round which organization coheres and which form its identity are rarely altered, except as a result of severe trauma, or training. For instance, a physical accident, like the loss of a limb or of a faculty such as sight, will compel not only a physical reorganization, but some degree of emotional and conceptual reorganization as well. New ways of bodily operation have to be learnt, for example, or the other senses developed to compensate for the loss. In addition, emotional adjustments have to be made, perhaps in the nature of accepting the change without bitterness and despair. Finally, a person's values and outlook on life may be considerably shaken up by the event and its consequences, forcing much re-thinking.

All this can represent the positive aspect of suffering and loss. Indeed, there are people who eventually come to be almost grateful for what has happened to them. They have lost something which was precious, but may have gained a richer life from the profound reorganization and new capacities which they discover in themselves.

Such a psychological change cannot be brought about by ideas, nor by the desire for change alone, because much of one's internal organization is unconscious. If it is not a result of the ramifications of traumatic shock, which may or may not be positive, then reorganization of this kind requires a gradual process of training, based on an understanding of consciousness.

The crystallization of a personal world, which occurs naturally with normal maturity, is inevitable but also imprisoning. It is all a question of how wide the boundaries are. Meditation is a process of gradually reorganizing each of the three levels of being, extending and unlocking capacities in each, so that the meditator may stand as a new being in a new universe.

The three sections of the book reflect the threefold human structure. The first section covers the physical aspects of the meditative discipline, both bodily and environmental. The second section explores the ways in which meditation affects emotional life. The third deals with the conceptual re-ordering which sustained meditation brings about.

To become more of what it means to be human, the height and breadth and depth of it, all three levels of functioning must be involved. It is not achieved through ideas, however subtle, however passionately pursued. This book, any book, can only offer ideas on the subject, which become translated into reality only to the extent that they are made meaningful and found to be useful in the experience of meditating.

When it comes to meditation, having a lot of ideas about it can be decidedly unhelpful. It is hoped that this attempt to distil the *essence* of the art will help rather than hinder the practice of it. Nothing which this book contains is intended to be taken as dogma. Assessment or verification is through experience. You the individual, learned or unlearned, are capable of acquiring the wisdom of meditation.

Prelude

In the beginning there is chaos and waters cover the land. In these internal seas many survive happily, buoyed up by this or that task, this or that objective. Others are drowning in their feelings or meaninglessness. Yet others build intricate platforms of commitments and concepts, which seem stable enough, until a wave from nowhere smashes the construction into matchsticks.

The possibility for change enters when something stable and clear is discerned, however dimly. It is a star, something which is bright and constant in itself. It may be first glimpsed as just a fragmented reflection in the waters, but its presence represents not only constancy, but potential worlds, or even galaxies of experience still undiscovered, and vastness, energy, and all the mystery and power of existence.

Once it is discerned, a voyage can begin. The star acts as a fixed point of reference, a reminder of our highest aspirations, by which to set and hold direction. The next problem is to acquire a boat, some means of making progress. Meditation is such a boat.

Once the journey has commenced, there are a myriad places to end up. Some who set out will immediately encounter an island which is calm and stable, and will be quite happy to remain there. Others will come upon a variety of islands teeming with new forms of life and interesting potential, and settle for one or another. For others, only a continent will do, expansive, rich and various, and able to fulfil most of their expectations, and give a broad perspective on life and the universe. There are only a few people who, having visited most of these in the course of their travels, and acquired some experience of them, will carry on into the night, the proud galleon in which they may have started reduced to a small boat with oars in which they row by a still distant star.

Of these, some will gaze in awe upon the immensity of space and, with the knowledge that can be obtained from within it, call it journey's end.

Others will fix their gaze on the star with adoration, and see all life in its reflection.

And others will see the star, the vastness, and themselves as a unity, and merge with it.

Just a few, a very few, reaching this stage, will lay down their oars and leap.

Chapter 1

Meditation and Human Nature

Most people, at some time in their lives, have tasted meditation. Meditation is not just musing or pondering in a tranquil frame of mind, but neither is it a complicated technique, a type of laborious pursuit undertaken by spiritual zealots in a quest for superhuman qualities and states of being, in the way that approaches which aim at the achievement of 'cosmic consciousness' or similar elevated status seem to imply. Nor is it merely a relaxation technique, or therapeutic package for the relief of ills.

Spontaneous Meditation

Meditation arises naturally when the conditions are right, and people often seek out the conditions without realizing what it is that draws them to the experience. For example, one of the characteristics of such situations is repetition. You can imagine our earliest ancestors sitting around a fire and watching its flames licking upwards and flickering, holding their translucent outlines but continually changing, swaying and leaping off at a point into the darkness. When vision is held by watching the fire, words tend to die away into an inner reverie and, for moments, even wandering thoughts sink into silence and there are only the flames. When this happens, meditation enters.

The same can occur to a watcher on the bank of a river, whose attention rests lightly on the swirls and eddies of the current, on the perpetual fans of water round rocks in the stream, on the slow procession of leaves floating into and out of vision.

The combination of the sight and the steady sound of rushing water may produce a similar effect by a waterfall; or if your attention is caught by a repeated sound such as the cooing of a dove in the morning, a soft little sound always the same, yet always subtly different. There are forms of music, notably Eastern modes, or Gregorian chant, which lend themselves to inducing meditation; music without distinct melodic lines, which carries on and on without seeming to arrive anywhere in particular, but in which the notes and patterns are always fresh to an ear which hears them with a relaxed, alert attention. The experience differs from being lulled into a light stupor, or doze, and no emotion, as it is commonly considered, is present. Music which raises a strong emotional response can produce a temporary state of heightened energy and feeling, but this is not meditation.

Some types of rhythmical movement are linked to natural meditation. Swinging or rocking – whether in a rocking chair or in the rhythmic sway of Jewish prayer – is an instinctive action conducive to it. Walking is another, and many a dedicated walker or rambler knows the state which can arise after hours of solitary walking when the internal monologue is finally exhausted and the steady plodding of the feet takes place in an internal silence. The senses are actually very acute, and the cry of a bird overhead strikes into the silence as if laden with significance. There is a sense of everything being full of meaning, poised and about to be grasped. Then you think about it, and instantly the familiar self reasserts, your usual thought processes return, and suddenly you are hungry, or in fact rather tired and looking forward to reaching your destination.

But that brief space when it seemed 'you' were not there, and only the world was, has fed something, rejuvenated a nameless part in a way which makes the day worthwhile and slightly wonderful. 'You' were present doing the watching, but as an objective observer, part of, yet apart from, that observed. All the trappings of your personality and personal view, which normally interpose between that which sees and that which is seen, had somehow dropped away. Suddenly a more essential You, different from your personality, was seeing, and essence beheld essence.

The Mechanism

There are certain conditions which facilitate such instances of spontaneous meditation. The body tends to be out of its normal patterns, either very relaxed or wearied. This affects the rhythm of the breath, which in turn calms the feelings, and establishes an emotionally tranquil and receptive state. In addition, there is usually some form of repetitious stimulus which acts as a device for side-stepping the continuous mental babble of associative trains of thought and feeling which occupy any unconcentrated mind.

This internal babbling constitutes an obstacle which is very difficult to bypass. Anyone who tries to make his or her mind go blank quickly discovers that it is impossible to put a stop to the internal chatter. It has a life and energy of its own, and the more you try to quash it directly, the more active it becomes, as if you are fuelling it in the attempt. Try it and see! A more indirect and skilful approach is required, which amounts to wearing it out. The perpetual self-generating mental activity dies away if it is deprived of the energy which keeps it running. Energy follows attention. When conscious attention is hooked by a gentle repetitive stimulus and held steady, energy is directed to this place, and the associative engine runs out of steam. Silence ensues in what we ordinarily know as the mind. It is like opening oneself to a different dimension of experience.

The silence, or space, combined with steadiness of attention, allows a particular sort of awareness, not normally present when the familiar busy mind holds sway. It is a simple focusing, which is alert and open. The world looks different. Everything inside and out is subject to a completely different type of perception.

This is in no way comparable to losing one's grip on reality. Clarity and the *ability* to focus are enhanced. Neither is it the same as concentration, which focuses down to a particular object, and therefore narrows awareness. The meditative awareness is wide, poised and potent. Its focus does not need to have a particular object, but rather resembles a shaping in the 'substance' of the mind itself, a shape containing silence and perfect receptivity. When the organ through which we perceive the universe is in this 'shape', the universe is not the one we habitually inhabit, and which we accept as 'reality'. Reality tends to be a name for what we have labelled. It changes as we alter the criteria by which we demarcate and classify experience.

Experiences of spontaneous meditation occur almost certainly to everyone, at some stage of life, though not all as full-blown as those collected in books which describe mystical experiences. It may be just a moment, quickly forgotten, when the world looks different, or an extraordinary peace descends, or everything seems to stop, or acquires an unusual clarity, or seems transparent and suddenly meaningful. It may be as momentary as the pause between the out-breath and the in-breath. For some people these moments bring about changes in their lives, even if they never try to recapture them, and would not know where to begin. Some may identify them with the religion they practise and receive a boost in their faith. For others, they are quickly buried as too strange and momentary to be believed, too unfamiliar, too unnerving.

Other people again go to extraordinary lengths to recreate the conditions in which such moments occurred or may occur. Sex can be used in this way, and mountain-climbing, exploration and treks through difficult terrain, sport, racing cars, testing fighter aircraft. What compels people towards all kinds of challenging, dangerous or emotionally demanding pursuits is that, under extreme conditions, the normal modes of functioning which shield us from immensity may cut out. Such situations knock out personality, and force people to the edge of themselves, the edge of endurance or the edge of death, where something else takes over. The results are well documented: a surge of power; renewal of energy; an opening out into a space of clarity, insight, carefreeness and detachment; intimations of immense potential, of joy, of peace, of feeling more and more alive. These states are of ultimate value to those who encounter them, such that they justify all the effort, and indeed the desire to re-create them may become a drive shaping a person's life, and beside which all other activities are secondary.

Maintaining the Meditative Experience

Such experiences happen when the conditions are accidentally or deliberately created. The habitual balance of the organism is changed into an alignment which allows new faculties of perception to come into operation. The mechanism which has been briefly sketched above will be analysed in greater detail in chapter 3.

However, experiences of spontaneous meditation raise important questions. Do they have to be so brief? To what extent are these meaningful states dependent on setting up *external* conditions? Those moments when a curtain seems to lift or be rent; when a thick cloud or stone rolls away; when it feels as if some heavy garment or set of veils has been shed – are they by nature only fleeting and fortuitous, occurring just when conditions can be manipulated or arise accidentally? If such experiences are so rare and difficult to achieve, they would seem to be rather irrelevant to the average sort of person leading an average sort of life! They suggest a sort of psychological liqueur, nice but unnecessary, for those determined enough to go after them.

If it is the case that some states of consciousness are operative only in extremity, or are so fleeting that they cannot be brought to bear on ordinary life, then indeed they *are* largely irrelevant to the conduct of life. States of expanded consciousness could justifiably be classified as optional extras if these circumstances were the rule.

However, there are two indications at least that they are far more fundamental to human nature than that. On the one hand, you do not have to push the body to its limits or dice with death to bring about a state of clarity, power and expanded perception. There is a much more economical way of doing the same thing, which because it is not tied to physical conditions also allows a more enduring experience, irrespective of circumstances. There is the art of meditation.

Meditation is a systematic procedure for bringing into conscious (that is, ordinary) life the dimensions of being which are part of our normal potential, but which otherwise remain unconscious, or are but fleetingly and erratically experienced. A changed perspective, and all that goes with it in the way of energy and clarity, can, through meditation, be sustained for longer in the life of an individual, and become more and more normal instead of extraordinary. No extremes are needed, no extraordinary conditions, and there are no pre-requisites of personality, skill, cleverness, or anything else, except intention and will.

For another indication that we are dealing with a deep-seated imperative, look at the whole phenomenon from another perspective. If you take an overview, it is not the *content* of unusually expanded states which is important, it is the fact that they occur. They occur universally, and, if you count the bottom end of the range of the most fleeting along with sustained states of 'enlightenment', something of this nature is probably experienced at some time by every human being who has entered the world. Add together all the scattered, isolated points of illumination existing at any one time, and the phenomenon is saying something loud and clear about the *normal* state of humankind. As a totality, a large part of our natural functioning at any given moment is in this 'illumined' mode. Reckoned this way, it is not extra-special, something beyond normal human function, but very much of the essence of humanity. The important observation is that human beings are *able* to change gear, to look out at the world and themselves from an entirely new perspective, and to know a very different world from the one they habitually inhabit. It says something about the nature of the world.

Instinct and Meditation

The deepest forces which motivate the activity of any living organism are instinctive. They are drives concerned primarily with survival, both of the individual and, more fundamentally still, of the species. Whatever a given species requires to ensure its continued existence is genetically programmed into the behaviour of individuals at a level which cannot be overridden. In self-aware beings such as Homo Sapiens, whose range of activity extends well beyond the basic eating, sleeping and reproducing behaviour needed for physical survival, the instinctive impulses work unconsciously, but they are extremely potent. A person may not be conscious of obeying a primeval urge to mate and continue the species as he or she searches for 'an emotionally fulfilling relationship', but the compulsiveness of the quest gives the clue to its powerful instinctive root.

The urges towards food, shelter and reproduction are inescapable in every normal human being. However, there is another factor built in to the program of a being capable of self-awareness, and that is choice. There is a variety of ways in which such instinctive impulses may be expressed. There is also choice as to the form and the level of consciousness of any action or behaviour. Therefore the instinctive drives may not be recognized for what they are. They may appear, for example, in the form of a need for security, for a home, lover, children, or for making a mark on the world through fame or creative achievement. At root, all these are expressions of common human drives, and whether we acknowledge them or not, they are active in directing each of us into the circumstances in which we presently find ourselves.

Normally they are not acknowledged, but simply form part of unconscious motivation. Indeed, they are very deeply unconscious probably for the protection of the species, so that they may not be tampered with consciously. The most basic drives can only be re-channelled, not obliterated. The constructive role of unconscious functioning is not only protective; it is also very economical. If the action of walking needed conscious attention, for example, we would not get very far very fast, and we could do little else while consciousness was tied up operating the legs!

The instinctive impulsions of a *self-aware* organism are rather more extensive than those of a bacterium, or even of a higher mammal. That which we call instinct could be regarded as an in-built programming for whatever primary characteristics are necessary to fulfil the nature of an organism, individually and as part of a species. The requirements for the perpetuation and fulfilment of human being are not only physical, but emotional and intellectual as well. All these requirements make up the characteristic nature of humanity, and all of them have an instinctive base. The drive towards emotional and intellectual expansion is as fundamental as that which has covered the surface of the planet with people. All levels of our natural drives must be fulfilled to ensure success in survival and proliferation. So far we have been a very successful species, but if we are not to fall prey to physical limitations such as sheer space, we must utilize and develop our other capacities to transform situations, so that we may continue to survive and evolve.

The name Homo Sapiens contains the essence of the drive most characteristic of the human species, and the one which distinguishes it from all others on earth. Sapiens is from the Latin noun *sapientia*, translated as discernment, wisdom, judgement. The verb is *sapere*, to be wise, to taste. Now there is a clue to the nature of wisdom, a matter of *tasting*. Of the five physical senses which we possess, only tasting (and by extension, eating) involves a transformation of substance. That which is ingested becomes part of the substance of the body in an irreversible merger. Tasting is the first stage of a transformation which enables growth.

The implication is that this capacity for 'wisdom' which distinguishes the genus Man from other life forms on earth involves taking in and transforming something into oneself, and results in growth. This 'something' is food for the whole being, and the growth implied is obviously more than that of the physical body. There is an urge within the individual and the species to extend the limits of the present state or conditions, whatever they may be, and to grow internally. In this is the promise of survival. Only if this requirement is met can we transcend limitations as they arise. Wisdom extends knowledge in a way which incorporates that which is discerned into the fabric of our being, into our attitudes, behaviour, and grasp of reality. Thinking about beauty, or love, for example, is not the same as 'tasting' them and, yet again, not the same as making them 'flesh'.

The wisdom/tasting aspect of Homo Sapiens summarizes that which is distinctively and fundamentally human, the ability to transform ourselves. It is imperative continually to break new ground, using experience as material for transformation.

It is the function of meditation to act as a catalyst for transforming and developing all the aspects of human-ness over and above the requirements of physical maintenance and growth. In addition, the difference between meditating and reading all the spiritual books in the world which also address themselves to this essential area is the difference between eating a three-course meal and reading countless cook-books. Even if, at first, meditation is not so much like eating a three-course meal as like nibbling a few grains of rice, those few grains taken daily are enough to sustain and keep alive the internal human body and gradually accustom it to richer fare.

The Role of Choice

The existence of the state which we call meditation is as natural to human beings as any other state, although it is less common. The concept of a 'state' refers to the physical and psychological condition of the whole organism at a given time. Far more familiar to most of us are states of aggression, passion, joy, fear, frustration, intellectual excitement, and the rest. The potential for experiencing all these states is deeply implanted in the composite and complex being we call human. All are expressions of the range of potential offered by being human, but no person is *compelled*, as it were driven by his or her 'nature', to be taken over by any of these, contrary to popular belief. That you are in a state of anger, for example, may explain but is not an excuse for any action. It may be easier to accept that, likewise, no-one is compelled to expand or develop any aspect of the basic set of components, genetic and conditioned, which we each have as a starting-point. The predispositions which make up your personality or talents, or the circumstances of early life which have conditioned your responses, are material to work with. You make of them what you will. The hallmark of self-aware consciousness is the power of choice, and it is inescapable.

Inevitably, according to the choices each person makes from early life onwards, some states will come to dominate and set the direction for that person's life. Aggression can manifest itself as worthy ambition, or as violence; fear can be turned into caution and skill, or become a straightjacket and prison; a glimpse of joy can be the stimulus for a motivating quest, or lead to a quagmire of sentimentality in pursuit of an ever-receding, ever-elusive personal happiness. Any personal characteristic, whether determined by genes or by circumstance, natural or nurtured, can be a positive or negative force, depending on the use the individual makes of it. The element of choice, the responsibility for making yourself what you are, is at the heart of our creative potential. It would therefore seem a crime against the species to abdicate from this creative role by considering yourself or other people as 'victims' of circumstances, upbringing, society, or any other external element. Even innate traits (in so far as they can be identified as such) can be considered as material to work with rather than dictatorial imperatives.

Just as there is choice in the handling or the expression of inherent characteristics, and of both innate and conditioned needs and responses, so the urge towards that which meditation can fulfil can be met in various ways. It can be dismissed altogether, acknowledged to some degree, or accepted and developed. Inborn drives are simple in nature, but the responses are very complex. Not everyone chooses to explore his or her fullest possibilities.

The Universality of the Creative Impulse

However, every culture of every age, and with every degree of sophistication, has manifested the drive which is at the root of meditation, although in different forms. For example, from tribal rituals to the grand ceremonies of state religions, humans create and look to some form of religion as a means of recognizing an expanded sphere of values, of greater scope and profundity than material well-being. Religions remind people of the existence of this sphere, which may be characterized as 'divine'. The creative dimension of existence may be personified as God or gods, and part of the role of religion is to maintain and suggest ways of keeping in contact with it. At the heart of every religion are meditation techniques, methods for establishing and deepening this contact.

People of every culture in every age have sought ways of increasing the tasting of life, not just by accumulation of experience, but by striving to extend it in depth, in meaning. Through religion, philosophy, science and art of all forms, creative energy is expressed. The degree of creativity in any of these is a question of depth. Sheer accumulation of experience is often mistaken for depth. Any preoccupation, whether it be travel, or sexual relationships, art, or scientific speculation, can stimulate the emotions, and through such activities many people strive to touch on meaningfulness by saturation of stimuli. Of themselves, these pursuits do not necessarily promote the shift where *meaning* can be grasped. Water, water and more water will never alone turn to wine. What is needed is the catalyst. Meditation is a catalyst for transforming the substance of life, for initiating the growth towards full human status.

Chapter 2

The Basis of Meditation

All types of meditation will fall into one of the following categories, according to the basic emphasis of the technique.

There are techniques which are based on *observation*. In these the aim is to observe with full awareness the particular object of the meditation. A common method is observation of the breath, its rising, its falling, the lengths of the in-breath and the out-breath, the changes which occur in it, the relationship between the breath and the whole body and the breath and the mind and so on. As observation becomes finer, so does the level of insight, and meditation is the result. There are many types of meditation techniques which involve movement, for example, walking, ritual dancing, some forms of martial arts, and most of these come into this category. They are generally performed slowly, in order to facilitate the quality of observation necessary for the state of meditation. Another form of meditation uses observation of the different mental processes as they arise. An important part of the technique is to observe without interfering in what is being observed.

In another category the emphasis is on *concentration*, and the object is to achieve steadiness of mind. For example, it may be holding in the mind an image or symbol until it can be kept there without effort. It leads to the image becoming 'realized' (made real), and this is only possible when the mind can be held still. Meditation methods which dwell on a particular concept, such as compassion, or attributes of the divine, can also be included.

A third type of technique can be classified as *volitional*, because it involves *willed* repetition. The classic example of this is repetition of a sound or phrase, but it can also be an action. However, the sound, phrase or action needs to be very simple so that the repetition can be maintained until there is awareness of the reality underlying it.

Any proper meditation will have all three elements, observation, concentration and volition. Although a particular meditation technique will be characterized by being predominantly of one type, there will always be the others within it.

There is a fourth type of technique often considered as meditation, although strictly speaking it is a useful adjunct to it rather than meditation itself. This concerns the flow of energy within the body, the raising and controlling of energy in the organism, and the activation of centres, sometimes called 'chakras', which can be located in particular parts of the body. Breath control is often used in this sort of meditation exercise. An understanding of these matters comes about naturally in the course of the previously mentioned forms of meditation.

Some Common Misconceptions

There are a number of activities related to meditation which are either called 'meditation' or grouped together with it in a general blurring of distinctions in the field of psychological work. As it is defined in this book, any practice with a specific function other than the widening of consciousness is not meditation. Raising energy, for example, is not necessarily raising consciousness.

TRANCE, ECSTATIC STATES, SHAMANISM

These use a repetitive stimulus to bypass the normal functioning of the mind and to give it temporary access to levels of meaning or power which are normally buried. Rhythmical drumming and dancing are often maintained for long periods of time, until an unusual state is induced. Consciousness is taken over by this state, in which material from the unconscious is drawn out; but afterwards it may be difficult for the practitioner to remember where he has been. Unlike with meditation, command of consciousness is relinquished, in order to utilize the powerful forces evoked through a particular rhythm, which is sexual. Among the countless natural rhythms of the body, the easiest to arouse and most obvious is this sexual rhythm. The first result of arousing it is considerable energizing. If the release of the energy is withheld, and it is controlled by a strict set of conditions and discipline, it continues to build. In essence, trance is geared to producing a specific high-energy state for a specific purpose, whether it be healing, scrying or experiencing ecstasy.

HYPNOSIS

The existence of phenomena like hypnosis and self-hypnosis, and the ability to perform remarkable feats like fire-walking, lying on beds of nails, or putting knitting-needles bloodlessly through the cheeks during ecstatic states, demonstrate very concretely the power of our personal world view. Our expectations determine what we are prepared to accept as possible in 'the world' and condition even physical responses. When such expectations change, amazing things are possible, as if a different universe with different rules exists alongside the usual. We live in the universe we *will* to live in. However, isolated feats of will, or giving over your will to another through hypnosis, are not acts which increase consciousness. They may have value in forcing some re-assessment or in shaking unquestioned expectations about the nature of the world, but what occurs is a specific and limited programming of the unconscious by a level of conscious will. Permanent change originates only from re-ordering in the unconscious foundations of our world view.

VISUALIZATION

Another category of activity which is distinct from meditation, although sometimes confused with it, includes various types of visualization. Some psychoanalytic methods and some forms of inner discipline use controlled and guided imagery. In a state of relaxation, the seer may, for example, 'go on a journey', and the details of the journey are revealing, and may be interpreted as significant in whatever context the visualization exercise takes place. Controlled visualization uses the associating nature of the mind to associate freely within a larger context, and while the conditions operate, a wider level of consciousness is being utilized. The images which arise are meaningful, but only significant to the extent that the interpretation is valuable as an aid to growth.

Through the skill of visualization, deeper levels of meaning than normal can be perceived. The power and insight of great art have a similar origin, but inspired seeing is like forcing open a door which quickly closes again. Something has 'come through it' which is potent or meaningful and therefore has effects even in everyday consciousness, but without a permanent reorganization of the psyche, the door cannot be held open, and the effects are therefore limited. Meditation pierces through both association and meaning.

REFLECTION

Often called 'meditation' are calm and reflective states of mind in which a person either spontaneously or as a regular daily practice takes time to reflect on his or her day, life, and activities; to see them in perspective, and to remember real values, especially when things threaten to overwhelm peace of mind. This is a wholesome and excellent pursuit, and many who manage to maintain serenity amid the hurly-burly owe it to a natural or acquired habit of setting aside time to reflect. However, although calmness is essential in meditation, reflection is not the same as meditation.

PERSONALITY

If reflectiveness is confused with meditation, those of a naturally reflective bent, believing that they are already inclined towards or practising meditation, may look no further into the question. On the other hand, those people whose personality is not inclined this way may believe themselves temperamentally incapable of meditation, which they associate with quiet, introverted types. Typically, it is 'Oh, I could never meditate – I'm not calm enough' or 'I could never sit still long enough'.

Reflectiveness may be associated with a certain type of personality: meditation is not. There are no personality prerequisites, and no natural abilities in sitting still or concentrating are required. The latter are generally the results, not the causes, of a person's meditation.

Meditation is beyond the compass of even the calmest, sanest reflection. It is an activity of quite another order, and the scattiest of mortals is as good a candidate as the embodiment of 'still waters'. Indeed, quite often, much better, because there are fewer preconceived notions and introverted tendencies to act as hindrances, and such people often take to the discipline more cleanly.

Meditation is an act of will, not temperament. This point cannot be emphasized enough. The only prerequisite is the *decision* to meditate – a decision at least to try, for a reasonable length of time, and to follow instructions precisely. True meditation is a deliberate undertaking. It is open to anyone who can find a suitable teacher.

Mind and Body

Breath is the link between the physical and the psychological. The whole area of breath control needs expert guidance or it can be dangerous. Manipulating the breath in specific ways will produce specific changes, because the breath is directly linked to states of consciousness and to the energy balance of the body.

However, the important principle for meditation is that *observing* the breath is a way to knowledge of the body and its connection with psychological states. All the different states of mind have a physical basis in electro-chemical action, and a change of state is accompanied by an alteration in breathing. It is noticeable, for example, when you receive a shock, that your breathing pattern is interrupted, and resumes in a different mode, or that in fear and panic the breath becomes faster and shallower. When you are relaxed your breathing is deeper and slower; tension constricts the breath. The breath is an extremely accurate indicator of the state of the organism at any time. There is actually no such thing as 'ordinary' breathing; the breath follows your state of mind.

Therefore it can work the other way round: your state of mind can be changed by altering the breathing. Some meditation techniques use this principle specifically to produce a state of calmness. As a long breath (deep and slow) is naturally associated with a calm mind, if you put the physical organism in this state by deliberate breathing, so the mind will follow. As the mind enters finer and finer states, so the breath becomes finer, and eventually becomes minimal, so fine it can hardly be felt or witnessed. When the body is functioning at optimum and is still, only a minimum breath is required to maintain its state, and there is a corresponding psychological state. Minimal breathing in meditation is sometimes called 'cessation of the breath' or 'prenatal' breathing. It is a condition which is rarely known except through meditation, and all proper meditation techniques lead to it, including those in which there is no specific observation or controlling of the breath. This fine breathing is an indicator of a state of fine perception.

Meditation and Physiology

All psychological states have a foundation in bodily reactions and chemistry. The most obvious and readily obtainable results of meditation are the same as those produced by any good relaxation exercises or therapy, which is why meditation is often equated with these latter activities. Meditation, however, is not an elaborate and time-honoured route to general physical well-being, as some modern, 'de-mystifying' interpretations would suggest. Regular meditation practice does establish good physical habits which are necessary for entering the state of meditation, but these practical benefits are an initial result and prerequisite, not the aim of meditation.

For example, setting aside quiet time in the day, away from habitual stresses and busy-ness, is beneficial in itself. In addition, meditation establishes good posture. Tightened muscles and strain in any part of the body become obvious and can be corrected. As internal stress is invariably reflected in tension in some part of the body, so becoming aware of and releasing muscular strain is a first step towards identifying and freeing psychological tensions.

To reduce general stress, meditation is effective physically by promoting bodily awareness, and psychologically by altering perspective and widening the perception of meaning and direction. In consequence, there are benefits to health and an increase in the body's resistance to disease, minor and perhaps major. Statistics on the effects of meditation which can be scientifically measured are easily obtainable. In brief, they cover such things as change in brainwave patterns (an increase in alpha rhythms which is associated with a state which is calm, relaxed, but not drowsy); increased skin resistance (a good indication of health); decrease in heart-rate; and lowering of blood-pressure at all times, not just during a meditation session.

Statistics like these give no insight into the nature of meditation, but they indicate to those who have no experience of it that meditation is an unusual state, which affects the body as a whole in ways which should be beneficial. They also provide evidence that it is possible to induce bodily changes at will, and this has major implications for understanding the physical/psychological relationship.

Stress and Chemistry

At the simplest level, meditation requires a calm and balanced mental state. Calming the mind obviously calms the body, and leads to a reduction in the hormones which are pumped into the system in response to stress. With meditation you learn control of inner states, rather than have them control you, so that eventually you can change your state at will as necessary. For example, if anger arises and you feel it is appropriate, you can allow it, but when it is no longer necessary, the energy can be changed and directed into warmth or laughter or tranquillity without any residue of angry feelings or churning emotions. The chemical changes produced by anger cease. This does not preclude spontaneity; it just means that you have more control if you choose to exercise it.

The role of will in determining inner states ('will' could be defined as the power which every individual has to direct personally relevant events, both external and internal; see chapter 6 for a fuller discussion of the nature of will) throws an interesting light on the question of hormones and individual responsibility; the extent to which hormones *cause* behaviour, or reflect it. Hormones are 'chemical messengers'. A messenger carries information but does not originate it. The two other parties to the agreement are the mind/psyche (which includes will) and the body, with its organization of functions. The instruction can originate in either and produce effects in the other. When it comes to emotional reactions, it is the mind which determines the reaction and the body which responds appropriately. In other situations, such as menstrual cycles or childbirth, it is bodily requirements that prompt the release of hormones, which have an effect within the psyche.

The important points to note are that hormones themselves are not responsible for anything and that the relationship between mind and body is two-way. Whenever mind is involved, nothing is predetermined; there is always choice. Even when chemical activity is originated by the body, the psychological consequences and expression, in the form of behaviour, are decided by an individual's consciousness. For example, the link between hormonal activity and emotional volatility may be inextricable, but the nature of the emotions and their expression depend on broader conditions already established in a person's psyche and life; how they are handled is under conscious control.

Energy

The primary source of energy for the physical organism is food. It is transformed by the body into the energy needed for its maintenance and growth, and for action of all types. It takes energy to move, and energy to think. The psychological 'body' also needs a form of food, which is the constant inflowing of impressions from the outside world. Impressions directly influence emotional states. They set moods, for example: the set of impressions related to a heavy, grey sky and falling rain are apt to produce a very different mood from the impressions related to a brilliant blue sky and warm air. And it is quite possible for these moods, determined by factors as inescapable and all-pervading as the weather, to rule actions and thoughts. Moods are related to how energetic we feel. A state of depression is almost synonymous with lack of interest, that is, a lack of energy to act.

Meditation enables you to make better use of the energy you obtain from physical sources, and it makes available extra energy by refining and increasing the psychological sources. Although the question is complicated, because energy is not a straightforward 'substance', it is possible to simplify a few general principles of the way in which meditation makes more energy available.

As awareness and perception are increased, so finer impressions are able to be received, and these are food for developing the psyche. Emotional control and stability, the ability not to identify with passing moods and to relate to an inner source of strength, all maximize the use of energy. The reduction of stress is another factor, because anxiety and muscular tension burn up energy uselessly. The less that is wasted in this way, the more there is for other things, including meditation.

Good posture facilitates the 'flow' or circulation of energy within the body. Areas of tension knot or inhibit this flow, which is another way of saying that where you are preoccupied and tense, energy is locked up holding the muscles in a state of tension. A furrowed brow, chronically tense shoulders, or a tightened stomach are physical reflections of specific problems within the psyche. Identifying these problem areas in the body and releasing the 'knot' will help to sort out the situation psychologically. The circulation and optimum use of energy are crucial while you are meditating, and they have ramifications for the whole of your life.

Drugs and Meditation

Any dependence on artificially introduced chemical substances is directly opposed to the essence of meditation. The purpose of meditation is to allow greater possibilities of consciousness to arise naturally and permanently. The body is quite capable of producing the chemical substances which are the physical basis of any psychological state, and relying on external sources does not assist the growth of consciousness.

Drug dependence is as much a psychological as a physical state, and while the causes which lead to dependence or habitual usage still operate, a person is incapable of exerting the will needed to maintain a discipline like meditation. With drugs such as tranquillizers and pain-killers, the general principle is that anything which takes the edge off awareness and fine concentration will make meditation more difficult, if not impossible.

With repeated use, these drugs and hallucinogenic substances also set up responses which can actually ruin the body for meditation. Mind-altering drugs provide an artificial stimulus for the manufacture of some of the chemicals which are involved in a change of consciousness. It is now well documented how, whenever the body is assisted artificially in the production of hormones or chemicals, it ceases to produce them itself and eventually loses the ability altogether. The natural mechanism atrophies, permanently reducing the possibilities of meditation. Conversely, the more the body's own abilities are exercised and made use of, the stronger they become. Meditation gradually establishes the electro-chemical state which accompanies the growth of consciousness, so that changes become permanent and integrated with the whole of your life and being.

Consciousness is not some diaphanous, insubstantial substance which wafts about in the brain. It ultimately comes right down to cells and their functions. Consciousness inheres in every cell in the body, indeed, in every atom of creation.

Chapter 3

Understanding the Mind and Consciousness

Why is Technique Necessary?

There is a question which occurs to everybody who meditates seriously, and which surfaces from time to time at every stage, especially when things are difficult. The question is: why, if this process is a natural one, doesn't it occur without effort, automatically, in the 'natural' course of things?

There are times when everyone is tempted to give up. Even though the goals of meditation seem so worthwhile and important, good intentions or even intense longing are not sufficient in themselves. Meditation actually goes against the mind's natural bent, so that on occasions it almost appears to be a battle *against* our 'nature'. Why should there be so much effort involved in realizing the riches of our potential?

Ultimately, it is the same question as the perennial problem of evil and suffering. Why are we all not good and wise by nature, and why is it that life and the world are not harmonious, in the sense of being free of conflict? Through meditation, an individual continually confronts this fundamental and ancient dilemma in him or herself, and is continually and actively taking part in a struggle which could be seen as the great archetypal battle between good and evil, darkness and light.

Growth in human consciousness, by its very nature, does not happen automatically. It is neither easy nor instant. Overcoming any limitations requires effort, but overcoming the constrictions which the mind places upon consciousness necessitates in addition a particular kind of technique. The knowledge of such technique is ancient and widespread. There have always been people practising a form of meditation, and the knowledge has been passed down and improved upon throughout the millenia of human history. By the very nature of the enterprise, only those who perceive the need for further growth are interested enough to take meditation seriously. For others it remains an area of no consequence. The knowledge of meditation and its techniques does not have to be deliberately reserved for the few; it is quite happily ignored by the many.

Aspects of the Mind

We must look more closely at this creature known as the mind. An embracing word like 'mind' is used to mean various things. In some contexts it has the limited sense of 'thinking' and 'reasoning', as opposed to feeling. For example, we speak of 'putting our mind' to a problem. In other usage it seems to imply the whole domain of conscious psyche, including feelings and emotions. Thus we 'make up our mind' about something, a decision which may be strongly influenced by emotional factors. In some religious philosophy, 'mind' takes on negative connotations. It can be equated, for instance, with the concept of 'maya' in the Indian tradition, the veil of illusion composed of the inter-play of created phenomena which the mind perceives as 'reality'. The veil must be broken through in order to perceive the absolute reality.

In ordinary usage, 'mind' stands for the whole conscious and semi-conscious psychology functioning in its normal way. It is this mind which meditation works upon, and it is useful to distinguish three parts or functions within it. Certainly it *thinks*. The thinking mind's activities can range from quantum physics to deciding whether it is more sensible to go to the bank before the cleaners' or vice versa. But much of what moves the mind is *feeling* rather than thinking, and you can 'change your mind' on a mere whim or because you don't feel inclined. What is more, feeling decisions often carry more weight than the ones which are reasoned out, for some people at least. For example, you may be offered a job which carries an excellent salary, far more scope than your present situation, and various other advantages, but in the end you feel that you would not be happy in it, and refuse it.

Finally, mind is not without a basis in the *physical*, and bodily factors influence the mind's operation. For example, a comfortable chair on a warm evening will facilitate a more expansive mental state than you are likely to achieve standing at a freezing bus-stop. You *think* better, because your thoughts are 'oiled', as it were, by *feelings* of pleasure and comfort arising from the relaxing sensations of your *body*. The three aspects of your mind are in a positive alignment. However, if the balance is disturbed by, for instance, bodily sensations taking over, you will very likely fall asleep, or into a mellow vacuum, useless for thinking even about what to do next, or for feeling anything more energetic than sheer well-being!

It is helpful to recognize this threefold constitution because it allows for a more realistic appraisal of the mind, and gets rid of some of the more foolish images of meditation, for example, of the mind as a sort of buzzing, obstructive gnat which you attempt to flog to death with a mantra or whatever.

During a meditation practice, the big problem may appear to be thoughts manifesting themselves as mental chatter. But chains of association, the type of thoughts, and the vigour with which they rise to distract you from the object of meditation, are conditioned by the emotional state you are in at the time. Emotional states play a significant part both in individual sessions and in your general progress in meditation. For example, it is more difficult to settle down if you are emotionally agitated, though the attempt to meditate is particularly valuable under these conditions. Long-standing states of depression or ebullience can also affect your resolution to carry on meditating, or how committedly you do it. Some people let the regularity of their discipline slip when life is good and they are happy, because meditation becomes less important to them then. It is a case of feelings taking over from the will to meditate. A physical toothache may be a hindrance to some degree as you try to meditate, but if you have a fear of dentists – an emotional reaction – this is much harder to overcome, because it may occupy your mind, causing you to be unable to do anything but think of dentists and molars, what will happen, whether it will be painful, and so on. A simple pain in the tooth is much easier to deal with than what the mind makes of it.

Every meditator has to cope at some time with the range of moods/states/conditions which are the human lot, but through meditation you are working to discover that part of you which is constant, and learning not to be pushed around by conflicting internal or external stimuli. Meditation trains you to observe thoughts, feelings and sensations, their arising and their passing away. What is it, then, which can observe these things? A feeling cannot observe itself, for example. The watching faculty must be separate or of a different order from that which is observed: it is consciousness itself.

The Associative Mind

There is an important part of the mind which works by association. When we are born we have no associations. A baby looking at his hand waving has to learn that it is part of himself – to make the association. It is by associating one thing with another that we make sense of the world. However, although the associative process is indispensable for learning, even when the mind is not focused on a particular task, associative mental activity carries on, without conscious control. When you are daydreaming in this manner, you cannot maintain consciousness, that is, the observing faculty.

It is easy to note when you are performing some mundane task how thoughts run on in an incessant internal chattering. One thought moves on to another in an associative chain which can be traced back step by step to the thought which started it all off. Just as there are chains of thought, there are chains of feelings. A feeling about something sparks off thoughts and other feelings which remind you of how you felt on a particular occasion . . . and so on. And how often have you performed a sequence of acts like moving an ash-tray, which causes the contents to fall on the floor, and so you pick it up, and go to get a brush and pan, only to discover that the brush is missing; so you hunt for it and in the process come upon a favourite pen which you lost some time ago. You pick it up and put it safely away in your pocket, but remember that the pocket has a hole, and so you put the jacket where it will be mended, and put the pen somewhere else . . .

which all goes to show how one physical action can lead to another!

Association is a very energy-conserving process. It takes no conscious effort to move from one thing to the next. In fact, it takes effort to interrupt the process, which flows like water, relentlessly, from one set of ideas and feelings to the next. Hence the idea of the 'stream of consciousness' is an accurate description, but there is no significance or meaning at this level of association. The thoughts which arise are like flotsam and jetsam coming to the surface of the mind. What surfaces is random.

The Role of Repetition in Meditation Techniques

In meditation the mind needs to be occupied, but not with material which will stimulate its habitual type of activity such as association. The examples of natural meditation given in the first chapter, such as rocking or staring into a fire, all have one thing in common, the element of repetition. Most meditation techniques utilize this principle, either by holding the mind on a repeating object such as a sound, which because it is repeated over and over does not continually set up fresh associations for the mind to seize upon and pursue, or by continually returning the attention to a single image, or by a repetitive movement. Holding the mind steady with the right sort of engagement, not too heavy, not too feeble, is a skill. Gradually the habitual associating thoughts and feelings are de-energized and no longer act as a barrier keeping us in the familiar world we each create for ourselves. The associating mind no longer dominates mental faculties, and the central focus of our consciousness shifts.

There is another aspect of repetition which is more subtle but very important to its role in meditation. The natural consequence of repetition is rhythm. There are many, many rhythms within the whole human organism. The obvious ones are heart-beat and breathing, but there are a myriad more, from very fast, almost undetectable rhythms, such as brainwave patterns, to the very slow: daily rhythms, monthly cycles, and perhaps, even some which take years. The body could almost be said to be composed of rhythm. When a repetition is maintained for some time it becomes rhythmical, and the rhythm corresponds with some rhythm in you. It could be the rhythm of your breath or other physical rhythm; it could be to do with your state of mind or emotions. Your meditation initially picks up a rhythm, whatever it may be on a particular occasion, and as your state changes and deepens, you are meshing with another rhythm which is a finer one. The meditation device is taken with it, until by finer and finer rhythms you journey back to the most basic of all, the rhythm of your very being. This rhythm sustains and joins one moment to the next, giving continuity to your life.

Employing the device of repetition prevents the mind being caught up in any thought/feeling process. The instant a thought enters, meditation departs. However, it is recoverable, and recoverable and recoverable, and the average session consists of a constant returning to the point of simple consciousness which is meditation, until this can be held for longer. Meditation is like an attempt to hover just above the surface of a billowing ocean, constantly descending to ride upon the surface, realizing it, hovering again, taking a tumble when a big wave passes, and so on. But it is always possible to return, dripping so to speak, to the place of meditation.

The Development of Awareness

Focusing attention on a repetitive stimulus, and holding to it, is a means of counteracting the associative chains of the mind. It does not itself prevent sequences of thought from springing up continually during most meditation sessions. But the process is inhibited and deprived of energy by a general state of calmness, and the energy which would have been used up in maintaining associative mental activity is available to the meditator to hold consciousness. The chain is cut, first by observing it, and then by not following it. It takes considerable and constant awareness not to follow thoughts, and to bring attention back to the repetition or object of meditation. With practice this type of awareness grows stronger and is more easily held, both during meditation and at other times. In itself the awareness is simple, colourless. Awareness is not the image you may be using, not the sound, not the movement. It is a power in its own right.

The quality of the attention or awareness that meditation needs and makes possible is the same, whatever the details of the technique employed. It could be described as wide attention, or the achievement of a balance between concentration and mindfulness. It is not concentration in the sense of a narrowing of focus, with the attention absorbed into something. On the other hand, attention is not scattered in many directions or upon a number of objects. The essence of a type of attention which is both focused and wide at the same time can be felt when you are aware of yourself attending upon something. The awareness of yourself as the doer is the ingredient missing from normal awareness. It is comparable to a re-membering of yourself, uniting separate 'members' into a new totality. (The image of dis-memberment appears in myth, for example, Isis gathering the parts of her son Osiris, who returns to life.) That which is normally scattered can be re-collected. The terms 'remembering' or 'recollecting' yourself are used in some traditions as a basic exercise for developing awareness, and meditation trains the ability to maintain it.

The Mind in its Place

Meditation techniques have evolved on a very practical basis, and all methods work on identical principles. There may be complicated or inspirational philosophies elaborating upon them, but the methods are basically simple and designed to get over the big problem of the travelling circus of the mind. You have to find a way to disestablish its dominion. It comes down to a procedure for 'sneaking past' it, by giving it something with which to occupy itself, while the self-aware and observing You, who are not the same as your mind, grow like a crystal in the space which appears. Then the mind, with all its abilities, becomes a useful servant. The function of a meditation technique is not to control anything, or to block anything, but to act as an anchor and guide for finding out more about the mind and its characteristics, and for bringing into operation faculties which belong to a wider organization than the mental processes we know as the ordinary mind.

A technique must be utilized until the practitioner is skilled in the ways and means of meditation. The mind cannot be suppressed, for it feeds and takes energy from the slightest stimulus, and if you attempt to work upon the mind using the mind, you escalate the problem and get even more deeply enmeshed. Know-how and strategy are required, and being a matter of conscious choice, they do not come with the birth-package. They have to be learnt from those who have themselves learnt from one of the long traditions of experience built up since early humanity. Personal experimentation without assistance is no substitute for this long experience, and the results are quite different.

Eventually the mind as a problem in meditation, chattering, restless, anxious, doubting, desirous and, above all, distracting, is overcome, but not by wiping it out. So long as you are functioning in a normal way in a normal environment, the familiar mind is always a factor to be overcome. It is impossible and undesirable to make the mind go 'blank': it has its particular nature and functions, which cannot be obliterated and should be respected, in their proper place. However, there are more subtle instruments with which to rule your life and evaluate the meaning of existence. The problem is how to discover the nature of these subtle instruments and learn to trust them, given the general internal clamour which will not just subside for the asking. Some way has to be found to silence the mind, and to allow a stronger presence to grow in its place.

In all techniques, whether using a sound, an image, movement or the breath, the action of meditation is the same. Meditation (a) bypasses the normal associative mentation, (b) develops conscious awareness, and (c) brings about a new form of organization in the unconscious foundations of the being. Meditation could be described as a method for growing in consciousness. As our consciousness grows wider and deeper a new perception of meaning in life arises. Those faculties we have which are concerned with fulfilling our nature as human beings begin to operate more fully and we may become aware of abilities we did not know we had.

But what exactly is consciousness? Does achieving the often-quoted 'altered states' of it mean the same as growing in consciousness?

Altered States

So often meditation is presented as a method for entering super-states, more laborious but safer than taking drugs. The thirst for excitement – for emotional 'highs' (what the medieval mystics termed 'sweetnesses and consolations'), for dazzling insights into reality which will solve all our problems and depressions once and for all – is in everyone.

Such states, whether they be brought about by drugs, or by exertion, or are completely unexpected and unsought, are inevitably characterized by a considerable emotional 'charge', especially in contrast to normal states. But although gaining access to the hidden splendours of the psyche is appealing and compulsive, it is also limited. If the pleasant states are sought for themselves, or are taken as a true picture of 'reality', they can prevent the development of deeper insights. Such states arise in meditation, too, but within a context which puts them in perspective, and counsels against placing too much value upon them.

Much of the emotional charge accompanying unusual states is a product of their novelty, elusiveness and 'suspended' quality. Ordinary functioning is suspended, whether for minutes, hours or days. When the special state fades, there is a sense of loss, and also maybe a sense of wonder and awe 'that it could be so'; inevitably, also, there is a deep longing 'that it should be so again'.

The key to establishing meditation in its rightful place – not a pursuit for mystics only, not a cheap drug, not just a pleasant therapy – is to understand that the profound feelings which accompany 'altered states' may be arising from emotional attachment to the experience. They are not necessarily in themselves revelations about the nature of reality. When a state is *normal*, there is no sense of amazement about it, of suspension, of its being short-lived and therefore to be hung on to; no sense of loss about it and no particular feeling of euphoria. In fact, there are no feelings about it at all. It just is: normal. Meditation can open up and make accessible dimensions which were previously unknown or fleetingly tasted, and make them normal, by making them conscious.

An Approach to the Understanding of Consciousness

There is much mystique attached to the word 'consciousness', but it is really very simple. 'Conscious' means exactly what it says: knowing, from the Latin *conscire*, to know. What you know about, in your ordinary state of mind, is conscious. In the totality of a human being it is like a band, or a circle, of daylight, in surrounding unconsciousness or darkness.

Every time a memory surfaces, for instance, it seems to emerge out of some darkness where it was still obviously very much present, though it may not have risen into the light of consciousness since it happened, possibly years or even a lifetime ago. Where has it been all that time? A full record of the event has been stored somewhere, completely unconsciously, and if you try, you can rake up more and more of it into the conscious band. With a deep and quiet form of concentration, or under hypnosis, minute details – which, perhaps, you were not even consciously aware of at the time – can be recalled. Having been recalled, the memory sinks back again as your consciousness turns to other things, but not so deeply this time. It is on the fringes of consciousness, or has been integrated, if it was significant enough, in a way which has contributed to the furniture of your conscious self.

Conscious and Unconscious

The conscious area is that most closely connected with the sense of self, and associated with the thinking mind. With our everyday conscious mind we slot events and feelings into the reality we have structured and, provided they fit without too much difficulty, we are in control of our lives.

But the conscious band is actually very small compared with the totality of a human being. There is a gigantic store of memories alone, accumulated at least since birth, most of which have moved into the unconscious area of being. They are still there, and given the right trigger, any memory can re-emerge. But 'unconscious' does not mean inactive, and all these memories, that is, impressions which have become unconscious, are built into the fabric of the person we are now, and continue to motivate actions, decisions and preferences, although we are, by definition, unconscious of it.

Since Freud, the idea that negative and repressed impressions continue to operate and affect current behaviour has become a conventional notion. Although it is a distortion of what Freud actually intended, the popular imagination has turned the unconscious into a sort of malevolent entity, full of dark and lurking shadows and repressed material. The unconscious, whether collective or personal, is not any sort of entity in opposition to our familiar conscious 'self', obscurely threatening because it is both outside conscious control and somehow working against it. The prevalence of a view like this leaves human beings disassociated from their deeper springs, powerless and nervous: analysts' waiting rooms are full of such persons, so are doctors' surgeries and community workers' files. Meanwhile, religious fundamentalism is flourishing as an attempted antidote to the same sort of insecurity, offering simple dogmatic beliefs to support the feeling that life can be positive and powerful.

Everyone is influenced by the prevailing image of what makes a human being. It is important not to entertain a view which omits the power and unity of human consciousness, or which encourages internal schism and the inability to take responsibility for all aspects of oneself. When it comes to understanding consciousness, it is much more helpful and more accurate to consider conscious and unconscious *not* in opposition, but as making up a totality.

Some forms of self-analysis give the impression that dragging out material from the unconscious, and cramming it into the beam of the conscious, is a way of extending consciousness. When this is attempted, the results do indeed seem to confirm the view that the unconscious is a sort of sewer. But any attempt by the conscious mind to meddle and dredge about in the unconscious is bound to be full of prejudice and value judgement and it also concentrates on the material most fascinating to the ordinary mind, namely, emotional. Thus pulled out into the light and dissected, emotional responses in everybody can look most unsavoury. There is no end to the minutiae of feeling and causes which can be analysed out, and more are generated constantly by the process of looking for them. Complexities tend to multiply, revealing more and more about less and less. This sort of emotional analysis does not extend consciousness. The beauty of growth in consciousness is simplicity.

The areas which are conscious and those which are unconscious can be seen as so intimately related that changes in one are reflected in the other, whether or not you are aware of it. The person you are now is a product and crystallization of all you have done, thought and felt from the beginning: crystallized memory in fact. To put it another way, the unconscious is actually *visible* as the structure of the person you are. But if you do not like what you see, and some of us do not when looking thus dispassionately, there is no cause for despondency!

How Meditation Alters Consciousness

Meditation transcends ideas and gives direct seeing into the reality of human being. The wider the 'band' of your conscious knowledge, the less in opposition or enmity your unconscious seems. It is all 'you'. There is nothing which needs to remain hidden, nothing which cannot be transformed into power.

A long-term discipline like meditation works on the totality of the being, with results that are both conscious and unconscious. You undertake certain actions consciously (the technique), knowing that there will be effects of which you are not directly aware. It is important to stress that the changes meditation brings about are unconscious as they occur. It is not a matter of trying to sort out or adjust your personality or psyche according to some programme of desirable changes. If your self-oriented and self-preserving conscious mind tries to reduce and order the internal universe into its own partial framework, it will interfere with the meditative process. You cannot manipulate directly aspects which are unconscious and that is why meditation is unique as a method of gaining access to and ordering the psyche. You must trust in the process of meditation itself, dealing with whatever needs to be sorted out *as it arises*. Change takes place gradually in the foundations of your being and unconscious changes eventually work their way into consciousness.

Meditation is a re-training process, part of which is the

re-training of psychological habits. Hence it has to be long-term, and fully conscious, which means that you constantly choose to continue meditating. You cannot meditate on 'automatic'. Once conscious effort ceases, inevitably you give it up. This effort itself trains, strengthens and extends consciousness. It may be that the area which is still unconscious in you 'contains' all kinds of abilities and power of which you are presently unaware. The concept of the unconscious includes a dimension which is greater than normal consciousness, a treasure-house of the psyche guarded by the formidable dragon of inertia and habit.

In terms of the image used earlier, the effect of meditation on the small circle of consciousness could be seen as developing the 'muscle' which keeps it small and enclosed, so that as the muscle strengthens, is able to utilize more energy, and learns the technique, it will allow the circle to open out. As more of previously unconscious knowledge and faculties become part of your normal experience, events are encountered differently, and in a wider perspective. Even events which before would have passed unnoticed now begin to make up meaningful experience and, as a result of this, too, consciousness is increased.

Present experience immediately becomes memory when the moment is passed, and constitutes the unconscious structure which makes you what you are. This in turn has bearing on future actions. In this way, increasing present perception will make for you a different future. The whole chain of human causality is affected, in such a way that it is no overstatement to say that meditation transforms the whole of life, past, present and future. What we do now makes the future, and what we have done in the past is built into the present.

The Simplicity of Consciousness

Brief excursions into altered perceptions and emotions do little to extend permanently the basis of conscious life. This sort of super-normal experience always becomes memory as soon as normal experience resumes, and although you may remember it, you may not be able to experience it again. If something is conscious it is, by definition, accessible in ordinary awareness, and therefore a part of normal functioning.

The essence of consciousness is simplicity. Greater consciousness does not imply that life becomes extra-complicated because you are able to perceive 'more' in the sense of a mass of information and detail. Rather it means the reverse. Consciousness orders and simplifies on the basis of meaningfulness and, as a result, ordinary life becomes simpler and broader.

The principle of simplicity is at work all the time because consciousness is omnipresent and constantly evolving towards the simple. Just to make sense of the world, your mind organizes what is perceived into meaningful structures which are based on similarities and previous experience, and related to what you think life is all about. Otherwise you would be overwhelmed by the complexities of life and experience. Most people manage to establish a coherent working structure to deal with everyday realities. Making structures is a process of simplifying, and the simpler these structures are, the larger they can be, and the more they can include and make sense of.

As an example of a successful, flexible structure or world view, there is a story of a helicopter landing near a remote Tibetan monastery some time ago. No-one fled gibbering about 'big birds from the sky'. The abbot, who had encountered nothing like it in his life, took it in his stride because his world view was not structured upon the details of the only environment he knew (subsistence living in an isolated society). It was based on principles which were large and simple enough to cope with the apparently impossible.

Another example of the benefits of simplification can be seen in the history of cosmology. The idea that the earth was at the centre of the universe, and the stars fixed in a sphere above, seemed simple enough until this concept could no longer make sense of what was perceived. Then it had to become more and more complex to account for observation, and crystalline spheres and cycles and epicycles were added to the model. The revolution of Copernicus was a change to a larger and simpler perspective which unified the observed facts in one sweep by a change of focus. With the sun at the centre, the model was simpler, more accurate, and allowed for a bigger grasp of the structure of the universe. You could say that collective human consciousness increased by a leap, ultimately making it possible to plot the trajectory of a Voyager probe in all its minute concrete detail.

The more essential the principles, the wider is their scope. If, for example, you wish to learn more deeply, there must be a shift from pursuing the impossibility of knowing everything there is to be known in every tiny complex detail, to understanding larger and larger wholes (or systems, or laws, or structures) which include more within them. Understanding a car engine is not a matter of learning the layout of every nut and bolt. With a grasp of the principles on which it works, the internal combustion engine could be reconstructed if every car in the world were wiped out and all the current mechanical knowledge with it.

Although ordering into larger structures simplifies experience, trying to describe them in a sequence of ideas is necessarily complex because language is a complex medium. Hence, although the object of this book is to simplify ideas about meditation, a genuine simplification of understanding arises only from meditation itself. Meditation goes to the root of explanation and is pre-language. It is difficult to convey the nature of consciousness, and of meditation, in a book which can only be ideas and theory. There are endless descriptions of meditation in the various traditions, just because the mind, of its nature, wants complex answers, but all these descriptions necessarily miss the essence. Meditation is a journey from complexity to simplicity, affecting in the end your understanding of life and of yourself. Meditation works by not allowing complexities to be the centre of your being, and by looking towards the bigger and simpler, gradually training the mind to apprehend in this way.

Pure consciousness is utterly simple. Meditation makes it possible to reach to this simplicity and hold it. Consciousness resting in itself could be compared to the flame of a candle. Every time a thought or feeling arises, and your consciousness attaches to it, it is as if the flame breaks up and scatters, diminishing the power of that central focus. The person who wishes to reach out to the highest (or to the roots) must aim to know the simplicity of consciousness. A useful description of the essence of any religious or mystical experience is the achievement of that simplicity of consciousness which can apprehend divinity in life.

Chapter 4

Meditation in Practice

We live on a small planet, relatively speaking. Most of us live on a small part of that planet, in some particular country. Within this, there is a particular area which we know fairly well and regard as our own patch, a state, or city or a county. But our actual affairs centre round even smaller districts, where the home and occupation are situated, and in the end our most pressing concerns are limited to our immediate family, a few chosen friends, work, leisure activity, and maybe a few issues about which we feel strongly.

This is unavoidable. No-one can be everywhere at once or concerned with everything. From this perspective it may appear that one individual is a very insignificant speck in the greater order of life on earth, a tiny cosmos of thoughts and feelings pursuing its own affairs amid the complexity of levels making up human society, local and planetary.

This may be the case, but it need not be. It depends on how big a human being is, not in terms of prestige or some measurable sphere of influence, but in breadth of being.

Being

A human being is, quite literally, much bigger in size than the form enclosed in skin. The latter is merely its physical body. Each individual being, however, extends as far as its interests and preoccupations reach, that is, to the limits of its day-to-day awareness. The things which make life meaningful for you are setting the parameters of your being. You could almost see people as interpenetrating spheres, overlapping where their interests and occupations come together, but each with a focus of identity which maintains its integrity as an individual being.

Some people are 'bigger' than others. You know when you encounter a really 'big' man or woman. His or her presence is not only stronger, seeming more concentrated and focused, but also extends a great deal wider, in an indefinable way. Contrary to expectation, a public figure, a politician perhaps, with a large range of responsibilities and weighty decisions to make for others, is not necessarily big at all, although there are some who are. There may be a faint, borrowed extension conferred by publicity and the attention of others, but these factors are no measure of the extent of being.

There is no objective standard for measuring it. It is a question of presence. Presence can be perceived almost like a field of energy surrounding a person. It is difficult to 'take the measure' of such people because they may seem to transcend familiar stereotypes. For example, occasionally someone enters a social gathering and nearly everyone in the room is aware of him or her. It has nothing to do with the person's appearance, or witty conversation, nor with extrovert behaviour, or any form of attention-seeking, but there is a quality of power and self-possession which compels respect. The qualities of presence cannot be counterfeited. It is not a matter of wide interests, but of a life and being on wide foundations. Having a lot of cosmic or spiritual ideals does not extend awareness, nor does diffuse thinking and emotion in any way 'raise' consciousness.

Largeness of being is difficult to categorize, but perceptible, and it is invariably accompanied by a life-style which is strong, clear and disciplined – for good or ill; it may not necessarily be turned to positive ends. A capacity for self-discipline is necessary because the energy which is spent in useless and self-imposed suffering, stress and emotional difficulties is the energy which is needed to feed the growth of being. Energy for living is a finite store, and much depends on where it is directed, and how positively it is managed. Suffering, for example, can either generate energy or drain it. So can relationships. The transformer is consciousness.

Living is a skill. The pursuit of excellence in any field demands discipline and the exclusion of much that is not relevant to, or that works against, achieving the goal. Indeed, the higher your aspirations, the more your life-style must be organized. There is not only a limited amount of energy, but a limited amount of *time* available, and neither can be wasted if particular skills are sought. The effort of self-discipline is even more critical if what you seek is not a particular skill, but a question of knowing more and being more, of becoming bigger as a person in the sense we have been discussing. The 'muscles' or skills involved in this primary enterprise of living more creatively are the mind and emotions. If either mental processes or emotional foundation are flabby or chaotic, they cannot do the job. The greatest assistance for the growth of being is a method for maintaining an overall direction, for setting standards and for resolving the conflicts of life creatively. Meditation offers a method of this kind.

The Role of Conflict

Living is full of conflicts on the grand scale and on the personal. It could almost be said that life is a study in conflict, from the struggle of saplings to reach the light, to the struggle of different species of animals to survive in the one environment, or of people aspiring to the same job, and so on. If conflict were eradicated, so would be life as we know it.

Meditation is not about avoiding conflict, or about achieving some sort of harmonious platform where the push and tug of conflicts cannot touch you. It is a widely prevailing notion that the peace which the struggling human heart seeks is of this order, but if it were so, the state achieved would not be one of more abundant life. It would be the imposition of an unreal desire, an idol, like resorting to the worship of a golden calf when the trials of wandering in the desert in the service of a living god seem too much for one's faith or will.

In fact, beginning meditation creates more conflict rather than less. For example, there is the conflict to do with time. Finding the time to meditate in a busy life means a continual re-affirmation of the decision as to whether meditating is really employing time more fruitfully than doing task X. The instant you allow a focusing factor like the decision to meditate to enter your life, it will come into conflict with your established patterns of activity, and with your internal 'freedom' to wander in every direction at the behest of your habitual patterns of thought and feeling reactions.

Conflict is unavoidable. You are continually in conflict with your environment in order to survive. Every breath you need to maintain your life destroys the lives of millions of micro-organisms; if you occupy a house, thousands of other needy or homeless people cannot occupy it; if you have a job, there are others equally well-qualified who cannot have it; if you do not have a job, you increase the pressures on others. And so on.

Given that conflict is unavoidable, you are left with a choice of making it constructive, destructive or futile. From constructive conflict life grows, from destructive it perishes, while futility is maintaining conflicts which need not be maintained. Every constructive/creative conflict has a destructive side. What is constructive for one objective is inevitably destructive for something else, but through a chain of balances and a hierarchy of interests, the harmony of life is maintained. Any ecosystem illustrates the principle, but the complication is that every ecosystem exists within and serves a larger one as well. Only futile conflict benefits nobody.

You will not have to look very far to identify an example of *futile* conflict in your own life. All kinds of internal agonizing, anxieties, chronic bickering and bad feeling, either within yourself or relating to others, come into this category. You will also see examples of *destructive* conflict without too much effort, when some project or intention failed to fully materialize: lack of money, lack of time, lack of will won the day and, like a small sapling in the forest, the development which was initiated lost out to the bigger, more established trees. Not every tree *can* grow in the same space, but as far as *you* are concerned, and your aim, the outcome was destructive. The mark of *creative* conflict is not only achievement in the face of difficulties, but also whether you learned something. If you did, there was a creative element in the conflict (for you). For example, even if you lose a particular 'battle', if you have truly learned something, the conflict was to that extent creative for you. Everything you have ever achieved will have been at the expense of something else. The achievements which are most valuable and meaningful have a trail of at least internal conflict behind them, such as the overcoming of indolence, or having to reject some other persuasive option, and probably external conflict as well.

Will

In the end it is your will which both sets and maintains a course of action. You may choose to do something, but the desire alone cannot carry it to conclusion. Other equally powerful desires which are in opposition to it arise along the way, such as the desire for more time to relax, or to spend with the family, or for more money to maintain a certain life-style. The extra factor which is needed to realize an intention, is a colourless, usually semi-conscious force called will.

It is not easy to identify will and separate it from desire or intention. What is it, however, which takes you to your saxophone practice or to writing essays as a mature student, when you are very tired from a hard day's work, it is a balmy evening, and all your family or friends are sipping drinks, relaxing, and otherwise enjoying themselves? At that time, desire it is not! Desires are always of the moment. Any apparently longer-term desire, or desire so strong it overrides opposing forces is heavily supported by will, and will is the machinery which brings it to realization. Will could be called 'colourless', because it is not influenced by feelings and desire. It operates despite them.

You may begin meditation for many reasons, with many ideas of what you want out of it, or none at all, but the only thing which will hold you to it over time is your will. Ideas change, the desires which motivate you initially will wane, and your enthusiasm will fluctuate. Such is human nature, and such things are inevitable (except perhaps for those driven by the machine-like energy of fanaticism. This book is written for humans). Meditation is not a crutch which will support you undemandingly in your problems. It will of itself create conflicts, but unlike many of the areas of conflict in life, meditation sets up conditions which always, by their very nature, can be creative. From the continued practice of meditation your being grows.

The growth of being expands and organizes mental and emotional life. There is no doubt that the world becomes a richer place, and that a level of personal stress and suffering is relinquished. The result is that calmer, profounder states of emotion are given a chance to be established. But it takes organization on the most practical level to keep to the sort of self-discipline which meditation involves. Being is not just a state of mind. It is a state of life. Being is recognizable not in what people think, or think they think, but in how they *are* and how they conduct their lives.

Daily Life and Seclusion

Does not all this talk of what comes down to a 'life-discipline' imply that one should devote oneself entirely to the practice of meditation? If it is so valuable, should not all activities take second place to it? Logically, it would seem that the 'professionals' who retire to monastery or mountain-top are in a far superior position vis-a-vis meditation, and therefore could achieve a level of competence in it which those leading an ordinary life could not aspire to.

Contrary to the expected logic of the situation, the answer to those questions is 'Not necessarily'. Meditation can be done on a factory floor. Ideal conditions are a help in some ways and a hindrance in others. In the busiest, most high-pressured of life-styles it is possible to make the space to meditate, and the benefits of so doing – such as the development of will, flexibility and control – may, in the long term, outweigh the advantages of having ample time and silence to devote to meditation. Every situation creates its own problems. Seclusion, or the narrowing of activities to those which are in sympathy with the desire to meditate, produces hindrances and traps peculiar to the situation: various forms of self-indulgence may creep in, for example.

Ultimately, the inclusion of a meditative dimension into a varied, pressured life-pattern is the greater skill. In terms of the growth of being, the wider the foundations of being, the wider its extent, and therefore the 'taller' it can grow. It is rather analogous to the principles of erecting a building or tower. If the base is narrow, the tower can easily be toppled in a high wind from an unexpected quarter. Of course, maintaining meditation without the support of external conditions arranged to facilitate it is harder; harder to begin, harder to keep going. It often seems as if you are trying to move against the flow of very strong currents, but as an encouragement consider the image of the salmon, returning upstream to its place of origin. The meditative journey is just that: a return to the point of origin, to the well-spring, to the point of creative potency from which we have arisen and continue to arise at every moment of existence. Living in conscious contact with this creative point is a whole new life.

There is no-one, in any situation, for whom this option is not open. Without questioning the occasional need for seclusion, or that it has value, it is the biggest romantic fallacy of any to think that the full richness of life is available *only* to those who leave it. On the other hand, the difficulties of maintaining direction without establishing special conditions cannot be underestimated. The sheer diversity and compulsion of everyday life constitute the scales of the biggest and cleverest dragon any purposeful knight could encounter. It is easier, some would say more sensible, to remove yourself to a safe distance and concentrate on building up your strength and agility for a lightning dash past, given that the 'dragon' represents a complex of attitudes from which no-one alive is exempt, and which have to be encountered and overcome on the journey to the creative. Mythologically, dragons guard treasure; they are forces which have to be mastered before the treasures of the psyche are available.

Withdrawing in order to muster your strength is one strategy. However, it has the disadvantage that until you begin to confront the dragon directly, you can never be sure of its shape. Knowing whether the dragon is really overcome is the result of experience in combating it. It may take more stamina and motivation to maintain direction in meditation amid the coils of everyday life, but the gain is knowledge. Your greatest practical help initially in this task is (or should be) your meditation teacher.

Living in special conditions of seclusion, silence or single dedication is an option which some people will always want to take up. For all kinds of reasons arising from personality, inclination, state of life, or religious allegiance, it is appropriate for them. In addition, the occasional retreat, for perhaps a week or so, can be very useful. However, special conditions are not needed for the full practice of meditation.

Choosing a System

Many people take up meditation as a result of encountering a particular system and being impressed, either by the philosophy or by a particular individual. For others, the array of choices is bewildering, while some do not even know where to begin to look. All that a book of this nature can do is offer guidelines for evaluating the worth or suitability of what is available, but the evaluation and the choice rest with the individual.

Introductions to various forms of meditation are plentiful, as a glance at the noticeboard in a sympathetic bookshop will reveal. One point to consider is the philosophical/religious background of any complete system. Sometimes the background does not matter too much initially, if it is primarily the meditation practice you are most interested in, but it may become more important later. If you want to go further in meditation, but find yourself not entirely in sympathy with the broader base, with the emotional orientation and allegiance as they are embodied in a religious metaphysic, you may be presented with a problem.

Another point is whether the system is Eastern or Western. Many apparently Western systems of meditation are Eastern in origin, adapted to a greater or lesser degree to a Western mentality. Again, this could become relevant as you progress in the discipline. Although the principles are common to all systems of meditation, the method, approach, expectations and terminology are rooted in their cultural origins.

Meditation in general has tended to become identified as an Eastern import, not only because the Eastern systems have only recently become widely known in the West, but also because in Buddhism and Hinduism the strong meditation tradition is so overt. This came as something of a 'discovery' to Judaeo-Christian culture as a whole. Here meditation has been more associated with the private or enclosed spiritual life exemplified by the professionally religious, or with the secretive and, to

Orthodoxy, suspect tradition of the Kabbalah in Judaism.

It is possible in some systems to adopt the practice without the background to some extent. Meditation in isolation from any wider framework is viable and worthwhile if taken seriously. Given regular and competent checking/tutoring, any practice is, in essence, self-contained, and can take the meditator to the core of meditation. However, the religious, moral and philosophical concepts do support and help to maintain the meditator in a way of life.

Some of the meditation instruction on offer is fragmentary, while, as was discussed in chapter 2, some of the techniques which are called 'meditation' are not. It is not that a modern interpretation of the technique which eschews any religious overtones is necessarily wrong or unhelpful, especially if its main claim is to do with relaxation and coping with stress. It may, however, be limited in its scope, and offer little assistance in extending consciousness.

Another consideration is that various systems differ in their emphasis. Some are specifically designed to promote calmness and tranquillity, for example. Some concentrate on inner power, and some may tend towards producing ecstatic states. The clue is the general tone and sort of imagery used to describe the objectives. Ultimately, you choose the emphasis which appeals most, but it is worth bearing in mind that any description of the objectives is partial and limited. You can always go further into the essence of meditation, no matter what stage or state you reach.

It is impossible for someone without experience of meditation to evaluate the worth, or to weigh up, in any degree, the details of the techniques and their effects, by intellectual grasp or by common-sense. You can only make an intelligent appraisal by looking at the people involved, and feeling whether you are basically in sympathy with the expressed objectives. Beware of your own attraction to exotica, which may have more to do with romantic leanings than meditation, and towards charisma, especially if it is obvious or ostentatious.

The fruit of a meditation system is the people it produces. This point is relevant when considering schools and types of meditation. It is not a question of how nice they are as people, but rather of the quality of their lives and aspirations, their integrity and strength. These are far more revealing criteria than a lot of verbal conviction or rapturous feeling. One should be wary of judging the system on the basis of one or two individuals, but a large number of people give some indication, partly of the product, but at the very least of the type of people who are attracted to the goals of that method. It is a help to observe with this in mind before committing yourself.

Once you have chosen a system, meditation is a matter of intelligent trust and self-discipline. A so-called 'critical approach', which is almost invariably a euphemism for the inability to trust either others or yourself, will get you literally nowhere. For the sort of changes which meditation brings about, it is necessary to put yourself on the line and do it 'whole-heartedly', which by no means implies gullibility or leaving your intelligence outside the door. Rather it demands developing an intelligent heart.

In addition, you will not discover more of what meditation is about by sampling numerous systems. For people who switch from one to another in an effort to find one which fulfils their expectations, meditation remains a closed door. Any valid technique can take you a long way, but only with time and commitment. Changing your method needs careful and serious consideration.

Learning

Why is a teacher necessary? Why not just learn from a book, or follow your own ideas?

Meditation is a process of training the mind, and a skill of high order. As with any skill, especially one which takes a long time to master, there are various reasons why learning from one who has experience is the most economical procedure. Relying on trial and error alone, in anything where there is a body of knowledge and teaching available, is grossly wasteful of time and energy and does not guarantee any but the most minimal results. Attempting to teach yourself creates problems of misinterpretation and you are likely to acquire bad habits which you are unable to see or correct for yourself. Once they are ingrained, it is difficult to eradicate them, and they prevent progress to a higher level of competence. A skill is not just a matter of knowing the theory, or understanding the principles. It has to be built in to functioning, and this takes time and practice. No matter how self-motivated you are, the existence of an external stimulus, guide, assessor and reassurer may make the difference between carrying on to achievement or not.

Where meditation is concerned, all the problems of self-teaching are magnified because it is not a physical skill, but a psychological one. The byways and pitfalls are legion. You are dealing with your own mind, and like the back of your neck, it cannot be seen without assistance. Nor is there a steady progression of easily identifiable results to bolster your motivation, or if there are, you are probably down a byway. You may further your psychic powers, for instance, without necessarily extending greatly your level of consciousness.

Every person is different. There is no set formula for checking on progress or seeing what someone needs in order to take the next step. No book or biofeedback device can substitute for the experience of a teacher, or provide advice geared to the needs of an individual, and this is absolutely essential for moving competently in the terrain of consciousness.

Teaching

Teachers or instructors are representatives of their tradition. It probably takes a few years before a person can be said to reflect in his or her being the philosophy or practice which he or she verbally espouses, but from a teacher you should gain some idea of the quality and flavour of the particular tradition. The ability to inspire with a magnificent philosophical grasp or articulation, or to convince you with a profound belief in the merits and benefits of their system, is no proof of any value.

With time, meditation finds out most of the problem areas in a person's life, and causes many initially ardent practitioners to fall by the wayside for one reason or another. If someone has maintained the practice for a number of years, as should be the case with an instructor, then his or her life must reflect it, for good or ill. The ability to maintain stable personal relationships, and to carry out personal and social responsibilities are positive indications, whereas if you see that a teacher of meditation is able to be flattered or easily offended, sets value on personal esteem, lacks integrity in financial affairs, or is chronically anxious or depressed, you have indications more concrete than trying to evaluate his or her 'being'. However, the main thing is to trust his or her competence in meditation. Personality is not particularly relevant; you do not have to feel a great personal liking for or affinity with your teacher, only a sense of trust or respect for what he or she represents. If it is a well-established school of meditation, you will be linking into the *school* and its tradition through the teacher, and the personality of the teacher is much less important than the teaching itself. Until you have chosen and accepted a discipline, if you should feel an instinctive antipathy, trust your instincts. And be wary of the charismatic teacher who says a lot, but doesn't actually *listen* to you.

Once you make your decision to begin meditating, you will receive precise instructions, and there should be a continuing procedure of checking or reporting to take care of the problems which arise, especially practical ones. However, it is possible to give some general advice on the practicalities, which should apply to almost any type of meditation except, perhaps, those involving movement. Even in movement meditation, the principles of the internal attitude are the same. Basic requirements like the need for continuity are relevant to all types of meditation, and the same sort of general problems can arise in any.

Place and Time

You should try to meditate in a place which is quiet and free from interruptions. Quiet is not always achievable, and not essential, but it is a big help. The sounds which are most likely to catch your attention and draw it away from meditation are the human voice, speaking or singing, and loud noise such as pneumatic drills outside your window. Background noise like traffic, general street sounds, or family life outside the room is not usually difficult to handle. When something does catch your attention, you simply note it, then bring attention back to the object of meditation, as often as need be.

Preventing interruptions is part of setting up the conditions. When you go to a private place to meditate, you need to arrange with the other members of the household that you will not be interrupted for that time, unless it is for a matter of real urgency. Phone-calls are very rarely urgent, for example.

It is sometimes recommended that you make a special place, with whatever ingredients will set it apart for you: incense, soft lighting, a special decor. These are more likely to induce a state which, however restful, is not meditation, and may lead to an emotional attachment so that you cannot 'get the right feeling' without them. Meditation is not a matter of feeling. A place regularly used for meditation does become special, and it is a good idea to have a place which is arranged to facilitate good posture and concentration, and which becomes associated with meditation for you. But sensory effects are not needed to achieve this. Background music, like pneumatic drills, is a factor to be overcome. Relative quiet, light which does not glare, and suitable chair/cushions/space are ideal, but meditation need not be tied to any set of conditions. Flexibility is of the essence of meditation.

It is important to meditate every day, preferably twice. Daily sessions are essential for maintaining continuity. Hours at a time are no substitute for days missed, and a spasmodic pattern, or meditating when you can fit it in, or for the length of time that appeals, will undermine the roots of your attempt at meditation. It is a good idea, particularly in the beginning, to meditate at regular times. Otherwise, in the battle between resolution and inclination-at-the-moment the odds are stacked in favour of inclination, as it is the more immediate influence. Will does not operate by brute force, and maintaining direction is a matter of strategy. You set up conditions for yourself, and utilize your natural rhythms and habitual patterns to assist your objective as much as possible. If possible, establish times of meditation when you are reasonably alert, but preferably not directly after meals, when the body needs to be concerned with digestive processes. Alcohol and drugs are great inhibitors of meditation. Meditation when you are tired is hard work, but the attempt at least is better than using fatigue as an excuse to avoid it.

If finding a suitable time seems impossible, you should examine your motivation and will to meditate. No matter how busy your life-style, it is *always* possible to find the time to meditate if you want to enough. It may mean getting up half an hour earlier, going to a nearby church in the lunch-hour, shutting young children in their playroom routinely every day and insisting that they remain there till you re-emerge, meditating instead of relaxing with a glass of sherry before dinner, missing some television, forcing one's workaholic self to take a break, and generally re-evaluating the real importance or necessity of all those incredibly important priorities and habits which we set up for ourselves.

Keeping to the prescribed duration for a meditation session is part of the discipline. Finishing too early when the going is tough, or prolonging the session when it is enjoyable, undermines the long-term effect, because self-indulgence reinforces the grasping self.

Posture

The postures recommended in various traditions for meditation – kneeling on the heels or prayer-stool, sitting cross-legged, or upright – usually have the ingredient of a straight back. Variations on crossed legs and hand positions, all of which have some effect on feeling and balance, can be taken to superstitious lengths. The essential requirement is that the body is in equilibrium, so that a minimum amount of energy is needed to maintain the posture. This helps the breathing mechanism to operate at optimum. Both these aspects maximize the use of energy and help to maintain alertness and concentration. The position must not be sleep-inducing, but there is no particular virtue in being uncomfortable, at least from the point of view of being able to meditate.

The body also needs to be relaxed. Areas of tension will hinder meditation, and a posture must be found which does not place strain on any muscles, including those of the neck, and in which balance can be maintained in unfamiliar stillness for a period of time. In a stable cross-legged position there is a natural point of balance, where the spine rests upon itself with minimum effort to the body, but the emphasis on cross-legged postures comes from traditions of Eastern origin, from cultures in which the body has been habituated to sitting this way. There is nothing inherently superior in a cross-legged posture for its own sake, and the necessary balance can be achieved on a hard, upright chair, with judicious arrangement of footrests (for the short of leg) or cushions (for the long of leg).

Posture is important, and should be checked regularly. This is part of a teacher's function. Bad physical habits and areas of strain creep in without your noticing, and it often takes somebody else to spot the frowning forehead, the rounded back or the ramrod shoulders. These habits have their inward counterparts.

Common-sense will tell you what sort of clothing is not suitable. You will soon discover the effect of having something tight around your midriff, or pulling over your kneecaps! In fact, the best faculty you have for handling all aspects of the physical discipline is common-sense.

Problems

The commonest problem in meditation is the following: 'My mind is often distracted by mental chatter, thoughts, daydreams, memories of the past, plans, etc. I know I should be holding the object of meditation all the time, but often I seem unable to do it except for short periods.' Some systems actually analyse every possible type of distraction, with advice on how to deal with each.

Let us take an overview. First of all, this situation is entirely normal, and it by no means implies that you are an unsuitable candidate for meditation, or even that you are meditating badly. It is a necessary and inevitable part of getting to know yourself and your mind. The same applies to all internal distractions, or states which arise while meditating. Practice helps a great deal in learning how to handle distractions.

Perhaps the most useful advice is not to turn your mind into a battleground. Internal distractions are part of the process: you learn from the handling of them. Something in you grows as you develop the ability to let them rise and fall without your being drawn in or identified, and many arise for a reason. You cannot suppress them, or rather, if you do, they will pop up at some other time. Meditation should not be about suppression. When distractions arise it is often possible for you to *include* them in your meditation, without disturbing its integrity, and in that way they will be taken care of by the tool best able to deal with them: conscious awareness operating without judgement, analysis or identification. The distraction then may disappear.

Individual problems should be dealt with by the meditation tutor. Many will be common in some form to just about everyone who undertakes meditation, though they may seem unique and even insuperable. In this category are all sorts of distractions, exotic and compelling experiences, states of enchantment and disenchantment, frustrations and irritations, itches and aches. Other problems arise for different reasons in different people, but it should be remembered that in the thousands of years of meditation's history, even these individual problems will have been encountered and overcome countless times. When you meditate, you are never alone. Others are trying to turn the same sort of base matter into gold, and you become part of an enormous company of all those who have meditated before you. There is no problem which is insurmountable, and which cannot be turned into knowledge.

Chapter 5

Change

When the practice of meditation is well-established it becomes a habit. Habits are an unconscious programming. They are useful, but at the same time they can constrict. Most habits are established without any particular conscious intention; they just arise in response to circumstances, and tend to be maintained even when they could be dispensed with. However, habits can be set up consciously. When meditation becomes a habitual part of life, the first stage is accomplished. It is no longer an effort to remember to meditate, and meditation is integrated into your life-pattern to the extent that you are very aware if you miss a day for any reason. You have set up a habit of being more conscious, and a psychological reorganization starts to take place unconsciously.

This reorganization is profound in its consequences. To 'organize' means to put some structure upon, or more precisely, 'to supply with organs: to form into an organic whole'. The internal organization resulting from meditation is unconscious because, as it takes place, the meditator is not aware of exactly *what* is being structured. Only the setting up of the whole process is a conscious enterprise. The result is a new 'whole', a unification which is on a different basis from before. Your personality and talents take their place as part of a larger structure with a different centre of gravity, and become more stable and functional.

Restructuring the Psyche

Breaking down the association process of the mind actually restructures your world. It is impossible not to live in a world of your own making, and habitual patterns of thought and feeling continually maintain it. New information enters the psychological system which is an individual human being, but it is immediately classified and becomes part of the existing structure. It takes something very powerful to bring about any real alteration in the construct which has been established and reinforced by life experiences from babyhood to adulthood, as they interact with the basic blueprint of your temperament. A startlingly original idea with far-reaching consequences, or a powerful emotional realization, may knock down a wall or two or modify the overall plan slightly. But then the mind's normal pattern of reactions immediately takes over and maintains the modified structure as before. Regular meditation, however, undermines the mind's monopoly of consciousness, and changes are possible because there is a gradual overall reorganization.

Overcoming the limitations of what we think we are, through developing a wider, simpler consciousness, affects just about every part of the internal structure, both psychological and physical, in a slow and subtle transformation. The point of it all is to allow and nurture the growth of your being. The growth of being may be a strange concept. Among the more obvious indications of this sort of growth are greater calmness and non-attachment.

Non-attachment is different from detachment as it is often understood – a sort of remoteness or lack of involvement. Non-attachment is not avoidance, but rather the capacity to meet whatever comes as it arises, from a point of simplicity which is steady enough, and broad enough, so that you can participate fully without being absorbed or overthrown. Involvement in life and its complexities provides the material for the growth of your being, but the crucial question is how much importance you place upon these involvements. A more accurate word for non-attachment might be non-identification. Most problems and harassments, for instance, are of our own making, and the mind's capacity to generate anxiety and to get things out of proportion is one of its least endearing manifestations. It takes deliberate effort to detach your self from all the reactions and interactions with which it is interwoven, and from which normally you take your bearings. There is a natural tendency to *want* to identify with the things you delight in, and to reject the unpleasant, but both attitudes spring from identification with phenomena. A simpler, larger focus is needed for a permanent sense of self, one which is not controlled all the time by the external circumstances of life, and blown hither and thither like a leaf in the wind. Such a permanent sense of identity, based on the greatest you as an individual can aspire to, can be known through meditation.

The effects of meditation upon the psyche are long-term, and they cannot be directly manipulated. As mentioned earlier, the reorganization which meditation sets in motion is an unconscious process. The conscious aspect is trusting the discipline, following it without deviation, and without *expecting* results. Sorting out the psyche takes place when the small and manipulative beam of the mind's awareness does not meddle, in its ignorance and desirousness, with a far vaster process of reorganization.

Results you go after you may obtain, but it will be at the cost of imposing your idea of what you want upon the unknown potential. Also, it may happen that results do not seem to be emerging quickly enough or in the form you want, and many people who begin meditating with high expectations give it up because they are not getting what they want from it. Looking for any results will act as a constraint. There is no reason even why you should feel tranquil and inspired after an individual meditation session, although often you may. In fact, the sessions which are more difficult are perhaps the most valuable in the long term, and meditation is a long-term process. After some considerable time, change of a definite and permanent character will be evident, but it can never be said that *one* particular factor or experience is the cause of the change. It is like adding crystals of salt to a glass of water: at some point the water will taste salty.

Ego and the Sense of Self

The unifying point of all the many objects of awareness which make up an individual life is the sense of self, and this normally constitutes the central focus for one's organization. Behind everything I see, feel, and am aware of, there is an 'I' doing the looking, 'I' doing the listening and cogitating, 'I' making decisions, feeling about things, manipulating all the variables of my world.

Meditation requires, usually as a starting-point, a fairly strong sense of self as a basis for further growth. You may not be particularly aware of having a strong sense of yourself, and it does not mean you 'know who you are', or have any clear or articulated grasp of your own being or direction. It is only a 'sense', which will probably be expressed chiefly in your actions and life-pattern, or be represented in the desire for integration itself, a feeling or sense that some sort of wider integration is possible. If there is not a firm basis on which to centre awareness, consciousness is scattered among all the many complexities to which it is attached, and it is likely that the desire to meditate will never arise at all. If it does, it suggests that, at some level, you are motivated by a desire to unify your life and being.

Human life tends to be all bits and pieces, desires which conflict, interests which disperse energy in all directions and which never quite come together, opinions which make a lot of sense in isolation but which, when juxtaposed, do not add up to a consistent approach. Many people are not sure what they want out of life, or what they really believe in. When your life becomes more unified, it also becomes more meaningful. Driving ambition, a powerful sense of self attached to some desire like achievement or recognition can unify a person's life. One of the results, and benefits, of a strong ego is that it unifies.

But to what end? If the impulse towards unification is directed to further strengthening the sense of self through achievement, personal power and status in the eyes of others, its results will be no more than that: the establishment of a large ego with a certain amount of influence over others. It is still very limited on the greater scale.

In terms of the growth or potential of a human being, a firm ego is a starting point, not the ultimate goal. It is a first step on a greater ladder. A fragmented ego is a handicap whatever the sphere. 'Fragmented' individuals are basically insecure and use up much of their energy seeking external reassurance, praise, or admiration. Most forms of neurosis are symptomatic of insecurity at this basic level of ego. By contrast, a healthy ego is integrated, self-confident enough to carry out projects and take on responsibilities, secure enough in itself not to need constant reinforcement or praise, and able to look for a meaning in life outside itself. It is the basis of mature, capable adulthood, irrespective of personality type.

In some philosophies there seems to be an emphasis on trying to do away with the ego, 'surrendering' it, with the implication that it is an obstacle on the path of growth, an enemy of development. This view is based usually on a misunderstanding of mystical texts in which the state of union with the divine is described. What must be given up at an advanced stage of the inner journey is not the same as what we are recognizing here as the ego. Much futile effort results from this misunderstanding.

The Ego as a Foundation

It is helpful to realize that what the term 'ego' stands for is not *by nature* a negative thing. It is a hindrance only insofar as it usurps the function of a more essential You and is allowed to rule when it should be a servant. Your ego and personality are the means for relating to the world around you. Do away with them and you would be unable to communicate, except in the most rudimentary fashion. The result of attempting to annihilate the personality in a quest for a more 'spiritual being' is an incapacity to relate fully and truthfully to the world and other people. The ego, with all its personal foibles, never needs to be negated, only put into perspective. There is far more to living than bolstering personal esteem, as everybody knows, and that part of you which recognizes this can grow, and become more conscious.

When you take up meditation the *importance* of the ego, but not the ego itself, diminishes. Experience which is not centred upon personal desires takes a more active part in your sense of yourself and of the world. Changes come on gradually. You are never able to see them as a direct result of meditating. In fact, you may not even make the connection for a long time, because of the way meditation works, namely, unconsciously.

Meditation builds up a core, an inner strength which enables a person to act even against the dictates of fashion. You are able to act from yourself. It also becomes increasingly difficult to blame things outside yourself for the ills which befall you. Somewhere the knowledge is born that you are the author of your own fate, and that you alone are responsible for your actions and all that follows from them. For instance, you may sit down to meditate when all steamed up about something. If you manage to let that matter go for the time being, and enter meditation, there may pop into your head the realization that somewhere along the line, at some level expressed or unexpressed, you yourself created the situation, directly or indirectly. For a moment you know this with perfect clarity. It is fruit of the sorting-out process which meditation assists. Afterwards you may choose to forget it again, but gradually perception of the long chain of causality develops, and the realization that every action has consequences. There is a simple rule which sums this up: For every action there is a result. From one action, one result. From another action, another result.

Rather than looking for causes in external circumstances (other people, upbringing, financial situation, society, other people's wrong attitudes, bad luck, etc), taking that responsibility upon yourself makes life much simpler, and allows the possibility of constructive change. It is a position of integrity.

Morality

As meditation unifies all the scattered aspects of your psychology, larger patterns of meaning begin to become important. Part of this process is that moral concepts take on new life. Meditation sharpens insight, altering the way you view things. After you have meditated for some time you may begin to see inconsistencies in your own life. It could be that there is some disparity between your stated beliefs and moral values and what you actually do. You disapprove of stealing, and yet you use the office phone for personal calls, expand your expenses claim to cover lunch with a friend and 'adjust' the figures in your income tax. You may even begin to see or admit that your whole business or career has a foundation which would not pass an impartial honesty test. You knew it before, of course, but suddenly it begins to bother you. What can you do? The longer you meditate the more obvious such things become. Either you give up meditation, or you do something about them.

However, you cannot change directly what is past; you and your life are its product. But you can take action in the present, changing the standards by which you act now. This then creates a different future, the past has less and less hold on your attitudes and, in quite a real sense, you actually change the past because the totality of your being no longer reflects it. Only very conscious action is able to change the past. Eastern teachings call it the undoing or burning away of Karma.

Once you enter this phase of meditation, morality becomes less a conventional notion and more personally relevant. The question occurs more insistently: even if everybody else does something, is it really right for me to do the same? Real morality can be recognized by its simplicity and economy. The hallmark of dishonesty and deceit, on the other hand, is escalating complication. For example, deceiving a partner involves a lie to cover up. As the situation continues, or as time passes, more and more lies and care become necessary to avoid being found out and to support the previous lies. Complications then multiply.

Whether or not your actions would be judged immoral by others, or according to conventional standards, is irrelevant to genuine morality. Real morality is not a code imposed from without. Simple, strong actions based on an understanding of the principles involved and the possible consequences take less energy to maintain. They have their own momentum and truth, which other people recognize. That is economy. You do not have to waste a lot of energy being clever, sorting out entanglements, agonizing over slip-ups, or feeling your life getting out of control and endlessly complicated. The honest tax-return, however painful, is much simpler to produce, and once done you can forget it: there will be no awkward comebacks with the potential for embarrassment!

It is not necessary, and not possible, to know all the results of actions. The test of economy and simplicity is a useful way of evaluating the morality of an action, and then there is nothing which can arise in consequence which cannot be dealt with on the same criterion. Simplifying life in this way becomes essential to progress in meditation. The result is a simplicity which is not about eating nuts and brown rice, but is shown by an attitude or standard of conduct which is relevant even in the most

73

high-pressured life-style. If your life is a complicated mess, it is more difficult to rest quietly in yourself, which is the very basis of meditation.

Adjustments

The stage of meditation where these issues become relevant is quite a difficult one. It is a transitional stage when the discipline is well-established and integrated, the more obvious benefits have taken effect and the novelty has worn off. You will find that life starts to throw up problems apparently external to meditation and these require re-adjustment of your attitudes. A new sense of identity is forming, around a new foundation. But meditators take heart: it is a well-worn path!

Some common patterns in the way internal change manifests itself may lead to discouragement. There are also some dangers to be wary of.

It sometimes appears to others that a meditator is becoming more and more introverted and self-centred. This can happen, but wise checking by a tutor should take care of the problem. The need to avoid this situation is one of the prime reasons why meditation must be under discipline and guided by someone who knows the pitfalls, and can apply correctives when necessary. Otherwise meditation can simply strengthen the limited ego. However, much of the apparent self-absorption arises in this transitional phase, when there are difficult re-adjustments to be made, and old values are falling away. A person may feel slightly awkward until a new footing can be established.

This applies particularly in some personal relationships, when the meditator appears to be moving in a direction which excludes his or her friends. This will pass, though some losses may be inevitable if the relationships are on a basis which is no longer valid for you. Deeper relationships weather any periods of awkwardness and end up stronger, while new friendships on a different basis from before become possible.

There is a fear which some people have before they learn to meditate, that it will make them less sympathetic, that they will feel less, be less emotional; they have understood 'detachment' to be like this. True detachment, or non-attachment, actually leads to the reverse, for the absence of personal self-interest allows the heart to function as it should. However, the aloofness which may seem to arise for a time in some personality types is most likely during the phase when many internal adjustments are being made. It is hard to retain one's former zest for, perhaps, trivia, when everything is undergoing re-evaluation. Nonetheless, phases in a long-term process will pass, and zest should return with interest!

As life becomes more unified, and the perception of meaning and meaningfulness develops, everything which happens takes on more significance. Life becomes richer through this increased perception, but there is a danger of superstition. The realization that nothing happens by chance can be stretched, with the help of a little self-importance, to the reading of enormous significance into every event. The world may become full of the Designs of Power, issuing messages. Someone to remind you about keeping a sense of proportion and a sense of humour is the best safeguard as you learn the rules of the new universe you begin to glimpse.

Chapter 6

Emotional Growth and Power

Results

The three most obvious results of meditation could be summarized as: 1. Calmness, 2. Power, and 3. Insight, representing refinement and development in the three levels of being.

Calmness has a physical basis. During meditation the electro-chemical activity of the brain alters to a pattern which allows greater calmness, the practical benefits of which are manifested by a balanced outlook, renewed energy and less stress. We have looked at this in general terms and, for those interested, more detailed information about the physiology of meditation is readily available. Although for many people these benefits are paramount as an inducement to begin meditating, in terms of the potential of meditation they are preliminaries, a foundation for the rest.

The basis of *insight* is the development of intellectual faculties – of clarity, perception, the ability to relate, co-ordinate and to penetrate into meaning, and eventually to reach beyond it. Insight first manifests itself when the meditator is suddenly able to understand, at least in glimpses, all kinds of religious, mystical and mythological literature which was previously obscure. This is because he or she is now familiar with the type of experience which underlies it. There is no substitute for meditation in the acquisition of such experience. In the last section of the book the development of insight will be explored.

However, the foundation for insight is emotional, and when emotional being becomes clear and directed the result is *power*. In this chapter we will look at some issues which are relevant to the emotional aspect of progress in meditation. Growth in meditation is always a matter of choice. It is possible to meditate for years without experiencing the sort of changes which are the subject of most of this book if, for example, one's objective is no more than achieving calmness as an aid to living. But with this book's aim of mapping the totality of meditation, it is necessary to look at certain areas of change and patterns of growth which are standard, although they arise in many forms, each person approaching the mystery of human 'being' with the uniqueness of individuality.

Suffering

Growing in one's being cannot come about without change, which is often initially painful. Pain and occasions for sadness are inescapable in life, but they are not always seen in a positive light and used to further maturity and understanding. There is a way of dealing with the difficulties accompanying the need for change, and that is to make suffering into a positive and fruitful impetus for growth.

Conscious suffering is suffering accepted and put to work. It allows for no self-indulgence, or negativity; no feeling of being a victim, or hard done by, or of being an impotent puppet in the hands of 'fate'. All these attitudes are so easy to adopt that they may become chronic, and a way of avoiding the message of suffering. Just as the sensation of physical pain is a signal, without which you might leave your hand resting on a hot stove, the sensation of emotional pain is a message, calling for an active response.

Pain and change are inextricably linked. If suffering arises of itself, through an unexpected tragedy or loss, for example, it invariably precipitates all kinds of changes, outward and inward. Suffering can be seen as a *force* for change, part of the mechanism of evolution. Meditation is directly concerned with human evolution, but in the mode of persuasion rather than force. You may not be spared the pain of change through accepting a transformatory process like meditation, but it may be that brutal external shocks are not needed to push you in the direction of greater consciousness – if growth in consciousness is a necessity for your being. Great force to hammer a nail in a particular direction is not required if a groove has already been made for it.

However, all pain is an opportunity, an emotional fire which can be used to forge greater understanding, of oneself and of life, and to burn away the dross and limitations of our personal reactions and weaknesses. This may seem a hard philosophy, but it makes suffering actually much less painful in the long run, and it ensures that something is born from the sadnesses and frustrations from which no-one is exempt.

The Emotional Body

Conscious suffering increases emotional maturity. It is as if our emotional life is in itself a 'body' which can grow, or not grow. Meditation assists the process of emotional growth by working upon the emotional body. It establishes a focus, a centre around which new growth can organize, but it is not a focus *on* anything in the same way as occurs when you focus on an idea, belief or philosophy. Concepts condition thinking and feeling into a particular framework, probably already established by others.

The focus meditation provides is a sort of empty focus, and all the more potent for that. Instead of providing ready-made answers, meditation continually raises questions, continually extends the need to ask questions, to understand more, to deepen emotional life by re-considering values and the meaning of everything. Answers there are, but only those which come from your own experience and insight are useful for the growth of being. Another person's answers are like another person's lunch: interesting as an example of the possibilities, but of no help to your metabolism! Through meditation all kinds of new food for the emotional body becomes accessible, and the ability to digest and integrate it.

Emotional capacity grows under this treatment. You become not less emotional, but more so, not in the popular sense of exhibiting weepy, uncontrollable reactions, but in the sense of having a greater capacity to understand, to hold and to control emotional states rather than have them control you. Love, for example, is an emotional state, but love comes in all forms, including destructive, grasping, sentimental, unwise, and destabilizing. How the state which is called 'love' manifests itself in an individual's life depends on his or her personal capacity for knowing and maintaining positive emotional states.

The 'empty' focus of meditation is not actually empty, but it is different from having a philosophy, or religion, or some concrete ambition, giving direction to your life. It demands the courage of submitting yourself to a process, the focus of which cannot be grasped until it is reached. It cannot be articulated or defined for it has no form other than meditation itself. The effect is like having a temple within, a space set apart, from which everything takes its meaning and also its power.

Power

One of the results of regular meditation is the development of power. This may come as a surprise to some meditators and non-meditators alike, so it is worth looking into the nature of real power.

Power is not the same as force. You could force a round peg into a square hole but it is hardly an exhibition of power. Nor is power to do with manipulating others according to one's own wishes.

Power has to be seen as a means, not an end. The steam from a boiling kettle comes out with considerable energy or force, but it is not power until it is utilized to some purpose, like driving a machine. In human terms, the assessment of real power finally rests on the purpose it serves. Power tends to be identified with 'power over others', but such power exists only to the extent that it is accorded by those others; there is no power in a vacuum, and what would be the worth of personal power and charisma on a desert island?

A sense of purpose directs energy and it is this channelling which converts random energy into power – and generates more in the process, because the conditions are controlled and economical. When it comes to serving a specific purpose, such as the management of a large business company, it is the person who is able to meet the conditions of energy, acumen and self-discipline directed to furthering the interests of the company who will command the power to be managing director. The power he or she has is relevant to that purpose; it may or may not extend into other areas of personal life.

The scale of meditation is broader. Its compass finally covers all aspects of life, and enables a person to act with power relevant to every situation. The question of power is tied up with both energy and will. Basically, meditation increases the amount of energy available to the organism for creative action, and trains and strengthens the will. Energy is the raw material; will is the channel and focusing agent. We all deal with these every day of our lives, so it is worth looking into them further.

Energy and the Role of Impressions

What is 'energy'? It is defined technically as the 'power to do work'. With any organic or mechanical system, there has to be fuel or input from the environment to be transformed into energy. The energy is then utilized in some form of 'work', part of which, in a living being, is the maintenance and growth of the organism. The rest is available for other enterprises.

The fuel for the physical organism is food. By alleviating wasteful stress conditions which interfere with digestion, meditation makes the processing of food more efficient. With a calm and balanced approach to life, there is certainly less cause for ulcers and chronic digestive complaints. Furthermore, nothing burns up energy faster or consumes it to less effect than nervous stress. Reducing stress makes more energy available for other things.

As with the physical body, so with the psychological, but its fuel is impressions. In a constant interaction with the outside world, we take in impressions through all our senses and the breath. Sensory deprivation experiments have shown that if the flow of external impressions stops, the psyche sets about manufacturing a substitute internally, in a frantic attempt to make good the loss of input or stimulus with hallucinations. Meditation not only makes the processing and integration of impressions more efficient, but also improves their *quality*. Better integration and the ability to utilize finer impressions both lead to an increase in energy.

The quality of impressions which enter from the outside world depends on your psychological state. For example, depression and boredom actually reduce the number of impressions which enter, and this further perpetuates the negative situation. It is noticeable how rejuvenated you can feel after taking a walk out of doors, when a state of lassitude or boredom had begun to set in. The exercise not only energizes the body; a fresh set of impressions has refuelled your 'state of mind'. You feel more cheerful, more able to be interested, more equable and energetic mentally. On the other hand, if you go for a walk totally absorbed in your internal world of depression, very few new impressions enter. The rejuvenating effect is thus reduced and the chances of getting run over greatly increased!

Impressions do not need dramatic content; everything the eyes and senses rest upon is potentially an impression, but it is up to the individual how many of these are actually taken in and digested or integrated, and of what quality they are. If you are walking with a bored or depressed frame of mind still dominating your outward view, only grosser impressions have a chance of penetrating to jolt you into some interest and energy. A car overturning in front of you might do it; the rest of the street's activities will not make much of a dent in your self-absorption. In fact, the psyche can be literally starved of the food it needs to grow, so that it is necessary to seek out grosser and grosser impressions to receive any stimulation or interest from them. Hence people seek thrills, danger, drugs, etc, in order to rouse themselves into interest and energy, and a system which is conditioned to these becomes dependent on them.

The overall effect of meditation is to increase alertness and the capacity for observation. With clarity, a sense of meaningfulness, and calmness, the world is a different place. More and finer impressions can be taken in, things which before were missed, dismissed, or distorted by the internal clamour or resident mood.

The Link between Energy and Emotion

There is a sense in which the words 'energy' and 'emotion' are interchangeable as regards the human organism. E-motion is literally that which moves you, a moving force. Emotional drives can be seen wherever energy and enthusiasm are directed.

If you consider closely why you do anything at all, over and above the necessities for survival, you should be able to identify some emotional need or motivation. The emotional element is obvious in the area of relationships and family. It makes the difference between a career and a job. It underlies the 'home improvement' impulse, whether the motivation is to establish social status or to create a personally comfortable ambiance and secure environment. An emotional drive is present in the desire for mastery or excellence or sheer pleasure in pursuing a skill; in art and entertainment, whether they are aimed at stimulation or relaxation; in sport undertaken for reasons of competitiveness or fellowship; and, of course, in religion, ethics and all value-related fields dealing with emotional needs.

Feelings

Emotion is not only a moving or motivating force. It is an energy-state, the overall state of the whole being when under the influence of a particular emotional orientation. On the other hand, the term 'feelings' is used to describe more transitory reactions which are occurring all the time, even within a more general state. Feelings are often based in immediate sensation. We speak of a feeling of cold, hunger, comfort, etc. Some sort of sensory base is also evident in feelings which originate from liking or disliking, attraction and repulsion. A feeling of happiness, when it arises from some pleasurable situation (one which senses and psyche 'like' and are enjoying), will depart with the situation. If the feeling persists, regardless of whatever events and situations ensue, even imposing on them its own quality, then it is a state of the organism rather than a reaction, long-term rather than fleeting, and is more accurately described as emotion.

For example, the words 'joy' and 'happiness' are used interchangeably, but there are connotations which point to the existence of two different situations. Whereas happiness can be a warm bath, and 'getting happy' be no more than a night on the town, and 'the pursuit of happiness' often seem synonymous with chasing a will o' the wisp, joy is a word frequently used of profounder moments in life which are less personal or of a more permanent nature. Joy at the birth of a child, joy from a reunion, joy in another's good fortune, religious joy, joy from beauty, or nature or art, and so on. Underlying states, which is really what is implied by emotion, continue to exist even if they are not 'felt' all the time. Feelings are the reactions which come and go in response to changing circumstances.

As meditation begins to work on emotional states, feelings become less wayward and arbitrary, and are invested with less importance. They no longer dominate outlook and actions to the same extent as before. Feelings, changeable, often conflicting, based on reaction rather than strategy or good sense, and very 'me'-oriented, constitute a tyranny which is overcome with the development of more stable emotional states. Any state becomes more stable, and is therefore enabled to be much more profound, when the responsibilities inherent in maintaining it are recognized. Such states can be self-generated, not determined by external conditions, and, unavoidably, a certain amount of conscious effort is required.

Negative states such as chronic dissatisfaction, frustration or depression spend energy without replacing it. Likewise, living under the rule of feelings is very wasteful of energy resources. So long as one's being and sense of identity are tied into every passing feeling, opinion and reaction, they are constantly pulled hither and thither. All this movement, plus the effort of keeping oneself together and finding a place to stand amid the prevailing flux, consumes the normally available energy, leaving little free for something as demanding as the growth of being. Growth needs energy. Meditation works by tapping into an energy source which is not normally available, as well as by gradually building a point of stability, from which the nature of emotion becomes clearer and emotional capacity deeper.

Will

Lots of energy and drive are of little constructive use without harnessing and direction. They may even be dangerous: unbridled energy without self-discipline can cause havoc in your own life and in others'. Hence the stress in reputable meditation teaching on keeping the practice disciplined, and on developing insight and the responsibilities which go with it. This is also why meditation and religion, part of which is a moral code, are often associated. Without either religion or the development of morality, meditation is dangerous.

No action is possible without will, so what exactly is this? In simple terms, will is what keeps you on a chosen course to the end, whatever the demands arising along the way, and despite the fact that you almost certainly lose impetus at certain points, especially in a long-term process. If either the demands (such as self-discipline) or the loss of enthusiasm and impetus cause you to 'change your mind', to give up or to change direction into a softer option, your will to achieve what you intended was not strong enough.

When will is firm, it is able to meet the ever-arising challenges as they come. Therefore it cannot be rigid. Will is not at all the same thing as powerful desire, or wilfulness. It is just as well, too, as there is a mysterious dimension to will: it can alter events in the seemingly external world. Will is a power. It is not always conscious; the conscious use of will only becomes possible in later stages of meditation than we are discussing here, but it is possible to sense it or to see the power of it in retrospect.

If you look at the underlying factors in any achievement you have brought about, you may discern some sort of intention, combined with a degree of determination and maybe an ounce or two of 'luck' in things going your way. All these are the hallmarks of will in action. Genuine will creates its own luck. Like most aspects of the psyche, will is capable of development as it becomes more conscious. When will is allied with the strength of a fine emotional balance and control, the result is power.

Chapter 7

Meditation and Religion

The Essence of the Religious Impulse

In Chapter 1 it was proposed that the instinct towards extending knowledge and wisdom is just as important for the survival of the human race as the instinct to satisfy physical requirements. One way in which this obligation to perpetuate fully human life is met is through the universal phenomenon of religion. Its spiritual, moral and social aspects fulfil an emotional need and they provide a structure to give stability to the emotional life of an individual.

To consider the *essence of religion* you have to lay aside the differences between religions, embodied in the various formulations and approaches, and look at the need which they all try to meet in their different ways. It is not our purpose to compare or attempt to evaluate religions as regards doctrine or institutional framework. Meditation develops the sort of understanding which makes it possible to respect the essence of each religion, and to acknowledge that fundamental human needs are reflected in the differences of approach between religions as well as in their common impulse. Such an attitude does not preclude identifying more with one religion than with others. Meditation is complementary to religion and should deepen, not threaten, religious understanding. Meditation is valid if you are of a particular religion, and valid equally if you are not.

Religious Feeling and Religious Allegiance

In contemporary Western society, a large proportion of the population do not practise a particular religion, for whatever reason. It may be because of a personal lack of interest in spiritual questions, or because of lack of support from the prevailing social mores, or as a result of disillusionment with the institutional aspect, or because of an inability (in a situation of having the choice) to find a religion which is 'right'. However, many of these people would be willing to admit to having religious feeling, that is, a feeling of sympathy or interest in the underlying questions, if they could only find a form for this feeling which were not one of the institutional religions which they have rejected.

Religion has an outer face and an inner face. The outer is its public face: group worship, dogma, cultural tradition, its ethical and sometimes political role, its institutional structure – in other words, religion in society. The inner face is individual spiritual experience. These two sides which make up the phenomenon of religion need to be distinguished, because people's motivations for rejecting or belonging to a religion can be based in either. The religious impulse and a feeling for what underlies religion pertain to the essence, not to the outer forms.

The impulse towards this dimension of life may not surface very actively in a given individual. Everyone is conditioned from the moment of birth onwards, in one way or another. Some are brought up with 'too much' religion, or for reasons profound or childish, take a dislike to aspects of it which they encounter as they grow. Others do not encounter a religious approach to life at all in their immediate, formative environment, and make no contact with it, and so they are conditioned to feel that it is unnecessary and irrelevant to living. When spiritual questions arise for these people, as they do, they probably do not consider them in conventionally religious terms, but nevertheless do feel that they are very important and may wish to pursue them. All conditionings can be overridden in adulthood by conscious choice.

Just because the religion question is so fundamental and so universal, no matter what society a person lives in, he or she at some point has to make a decision about it, either to discard it, to embrace it, or to maintain a non-committal attitude until able to be convinced one way or the other.

Two factors involved in establishing some position on the question are (a) conditioning and (b) having personal experience of a religious nature. The two factors interact, one influencing the other. When the conditioning is adverse, intimations of another dimension – the unsought moments of altered awareness, or even an unadmitted longing towards something bigger and more important than oneself – receive little attention, or are brushed aside. Naturally, experience of this order fails to grow into anything very convincing. Very few people are struck down on a road to Damascus by a bolt from their unconscious which they cannot ignore. Experience grows only if it is accepted and assimilated. Even if your nose is rubbed in some fact repeatedly, this will not become part of your conscious experience until you have accepted it and learnt from it – in other words, until you have made it meaningful. Opening yourself to the sort of experience which will make the deeper dimension of religion meaningful is a matter of conscious choice. The ability to perceive meaning grows or diminishes according to this individual choice.

The Relationship between Religion and Meditation

It is true that both meditation and religion create meaning in life. To a religious believer, religion is of central importance. It provides direction and focus; a standard of personal conduct, and an incentive to behave constructively; and a structure and language with which to understand life and to relate and interpret events. It gives a secure emotional framework which lends meaning to every smallest action and event, and it can transform negativity into something useful. Meditation has the same results, but there is a difference in the degree of personal knowledge. Meditation expands perception of meaning and opens a way to deeper and deeper experience. Religion offers formulations of the most important aim of human life – worshipping God, reaching enlightenment, surrendering to the will of Allah, following the Tao – to define what is meaningful. On the other hand, meditation offers a means of safe passage into the darkness of the divine where no images or formulations are adequate. In considering meditation and religion separately, it should not be forgotten, though, that some form of meditation has always been the key to extending spiritual experience and knowledge in every religion.

In the past, religion and meditation were accepted as part of the same thing. That is no longer the case. At least in Western society, we are faced with a choice of religions, and a choice of meditation techniques, offered separately, and serving different, though related, purposes. Some people are Christian believers but do a daily Buddhist meditation practice; others are Jewish and take up yoga. (This mixing of backgrounds is feasible at least to some degree; it may depend on how far you wish to take either the practice or religious conformity.)

Through religion or meditation, people are groping towards something which they feel is important. Even seeing meditation as an avenue leading to greater calmness with which to handle the stresses of life is a step in the same direction. In the West a situation has arisen in which there is a bewildering range of options and advice available – so much literature promoting alternative versions of the 'truth', so many claims to authority and insight in the sphere of spirituality. But, ultimately, all external answers to the most fundamental questions are unsatisfactory. Insight is not transferable. Only the methods for reaching it oneself can be passed on. Both religion and meditation, together or separately, are guardians of traditions for achieving individual realization. However, there are some differences between meditation as a method in its own right and the broader platform provided by religion.

The Role of Doctrine

When they are taught in a religious context, meditation techniques are a means of furthering individual spiritual life and understanding. They work equally well to fulfil this purpose even if the individual does not already have a framework of terminology within which to interpret his or her experience, that is, does not have a particular religious allegiance. Because the perception of meaning which meditation promotes is open-ended, meditation is not dependent on a religious background, and a meditator does not need existing formulations in order to integrate experience into consciousness. At a certain stage in the development of understanding and insight it is essential to lay aside all formulations, because they constrain direct experience. To re-apprehend the divine is an experience of true creativity. The experience is new, ever fresh, and it may or may not serve to perpetuate what others have seen and described before. If images and expectations are clung to, inevitably what is experienced will be seen in these terms and the formulations are then re-inforced. This may be at the cost of increasing the capacity to experience more and deeper, and so it may inhibit the essential creativity of experience of the divine.

Religions have an interest in maintaining their particular formulated statements about divine realities, as the entire structure of the doctrine rests upon upholding a particular view. Religions are characterized and differ from each other through these statements in the form of dogma or imagery, and sincere and committed religious belief does not demand re-apprehending such statements oneself. Unlike meditation, a religion is a corporate body. It is held together by an agreed format, a view of the divine which is accepted by all adherents, and by maintaining a common channel for relating to it. When there is a body like this, it requires organization and an institutional framework. An institution operates as a group within society, and its social role may have political ramifications. The consequence is a mixture, and sometimes confusion, of spiritual, social and political interests. Because meditation does not depend on doctrine, and because it is a method for individual realization, it concentrates on that which unites all traditions.

Faith and Belief

Faith is relevant in both religion and meditation. An attitude of faith is an orientation of the heart. It differs from 'belief' in that faith is an emotional stance, an attitude or approach which can be quite open-ended, and unlike belief, does not pre-suppose that its object is 'the truth'. Faith and belief may exist side by side for many stages of developing religious understanding, but they are not the same thing. Faith is a dynamic rather than a set of answers, and it can be consciously adopted and consciously maintained as a positive attitude without any particular content.

Faith can tolerate questions; it makes it possible to suspend belief and disbelief, and strengthens the will at times when the going is tough. The origin of faith lies in an apprehension of realizable possibilities, that is, it springs from a sense of *things which can be known*, and it maintains the incentive to work towards that knowledge.

What you believe in, on the other hand, you accept as true, as factual, although it may be without evidence or personal experience, or even necessarily understanding. By definition, if you have evidence or experience, you do not need to believe: you know. Belief does not demand or necessarily result in the growth of being: the coercion of fanaticism and fundamentalism both originate from sincere religious beliefs!

Individual Spiritual Life

If you look to the heart of religion, where it relates to an individual, there you will find methods for increasing personal religious life, and among these is some form of meditation. Ultimately, religion is about relationship with the divine, and the ability to enter into relationship resides in *individual* psychology. Group worship acts as a channel, and a reminder, and a re-inforcement for individuals. Sacred ritual serves the further purpose of embodying in symbolic action a collective intention. (The question of ritual, however, is beyond the compass of this book.)

Religious bodies can become preoccupied with their social role, with interpretations of how the doctrine applies to social issues and political directions, and with a moral role based on these interpretations. They may then attempt to prescribe not only how people should behave, but also how they ought to *think* on certain issues affecting society. This manifestation of religion is directly counter to the spirit of meditation. Meditation is an individual matter. Through meditation, behaviour and attitudes may be transformed, but only as a result of understanding the roots of them in oneself. When religious authorities lose sight of their primary obligation to further the individual relationship with the divine and to teach the methods appropriate to this, then the wellsprings of that religion are threatened.

It is only through individuals that the essential contact with the spiritual source of a religion can be maintained. Individual spiritual life grows through effort, and through employing methods of overcoming the psychological inertia which prevents the development of deeper experience.

Religion provides three such methods. Firstly, there are various personal disciplines like fasting, abstinence, regular times for prayer and regular attendance at collective ritual, all of which can be made more or less meaningful according to the amount of conscious attention given them. Even for those with no particular personal religious feeling or interest, these practices affirm membership of the religious group and collective identity. For others they help strengthen and vivify their religious feeling. They do not, of themselves, lead to religious growth or deepening understanding.

The second method of extending religious life is prayer, and the third is meditation. The subject of meditation is well-covered, but a closer look at the nature of prayer might be of interest.

Prayer

Prayer opens the heart and directs the energy of emotional being towards something greater than the personal self. There are three general types.

ASSOCIATIVE PRAYER
This category covers prayer in which the words are important. Conversational prayer, all kinds of 'talking' with God, is of this type, and one form of this is petitionary. It may not be quite as straightforward as: 'Please God, give me a bike for my birthday', but whenever something is sought, some object or benefit, or quality, the prayer is a beseeching. What is requested could be for oneself or for others; the prayer could be for strength, or healing, or peace, or even for the ability to love and serve God better. Whatever the object, the prayer has the effect of turning the heart outwards and establishing a relationship between the self and that which is greater. In this respect, such prayer always has results. It

may also bring about the object desired, that is, the prayer may be 'granted', but this is a separate question. Petitionary prayer contains a great deal of personal feeling and association.

This type of prayer can be spontaneous – composed by the individual – or 'formulated' – utilizing a set form of words. In addition, the degree of conscious attention is variable. Prayer which is recited mechanically does little more than maintain the intention to pray, but it keeps religious identity alive. Praying while thinking about the significance of the words and attempting to mean them does more to nurture religious life. However, both ways of praying are associative, that is, they utilize the mind's normal association of ideas and feelings, always relating them to oneself. It is prayer of relationship, needing the conception of an 'other' separate divine identity – an image of God. Associative prayer demands that the divine be personified.

PRAYER OF MEANING
This type of prayer represents a further stage, which reaches beyond association into the level of meaning. Words are less important, prayer is more formless, and personal identity less of a factor. Words are used as a continuous litany maintaining the intent and direction of the focus, while 'underneath' is a process of either dwelling upon images with emotional significance, or holding a silence in which a sense of the overall meaning is paramount. In this category is that which could be described as prayer of praise, the action of affirming the divine, of celebrating or extolling divine attributes, of expressing gratitude.

Chanting and some types of liturgical or group prayer work this way, and any familiar prayer can be used similarly. For example, in Christianity the Lord's Prayer can be recited associatively, thinking about the meaning of the words, or it can be said in a way which perceives the prayer as a totality and maintains an awareness of the overall meaning of it. The latter differs from a mechanical recitation in that, although in neither case is there much attention on the words, holding awareness on the meaning requires considerable conscious attention. This kind of praying is more difficult than associative praying because of the finer level of consciousness involved in a simpler, more formless level.

WORDLESS PRAYER

The next stage is to drop the words altogether, or just to repeat a few over and over, or simply to repeat a sound, which has no meaningful associations at all. It is in the silence which can be perceived underlying a continuous chant or litany that meditation begins, and the fewer associations there are to involve the mind, the more the silence can be known. Such silence is one of communion; of the heart at one with itself, or with the divine within. It is the silence underlying all creation.

Meditation is a development of prayer, into the formless, the simple; into direct apprehension. All religions have a form of meditation but, because it is a skill, it requires training, and this is sometimes identified with, or restricted to, the sort of training received in religious communities. This situation was reviewed in Chapter 4, with the conclusion that if meditation is natural to human beings, it can be undertaken in any conditions or way of life, although each has its own demands and characteristic difficulties.

The world, and the religious world, changes and moves on. The religious life of humankind must move with it. It may be that the patterns and organizations of religious life – customs and expectations which may have originated and been fitting in a very different society – have to change in order to fit the society in which we live now. However, all such changes should be based on the highest religious values and understanding, not be merely a matter of expediency or fashionable adaptation. The role of meditation in maintaining the essential values is crucial.

Chapter 8

Deepening Individual Experience

In this chapter we will look at types of experience which are to some degree extraordinary, and at the ways in which they are interpreted and communicated. Amongst such experiences are those which in religion are called *mystical*; others which are labelled *paranormal* or psychic manifestations, for which there need be no particular religious basis; and the experience which arises as a result of *meditation*. We are dealing with interpretations of a powerful kind of human experience. In different contexts this type of experience is given a different significance, and it may serve different purposes, but the nature of the power or powers involved, whatever the context, is emotional.

We have already seen that emotion is not the same as the feeling reactions which are often called emotional. Emotional life is capable of enormous expansion, which takes place when a person begins to question the nature of reality and look for a greater meaning on which to base his or her sense of self. When people have an experience of a larger dimension, it may trigger in them a quest for greater meaning, and, as a consequence of the search, experiences of this kind increase in frequency and depth.

People who take their religious life seriously, or who take up meditation, find that they are continually dealing with their emotions in a way which enriches their day-to-day existence and opens up new areas of potential. It is important to clarify the process at work in the psyche. Unusual experience is made fruitful for the growth of emotional being when the emotional energy involved is directed towards a conscious purpose. Sometimes the sheer impact of such experience is valued rather than what it may signify in a larger context. It requires a certain amount of detachment not to be enthralled by emotional energy.

We will begin by considering religious experience.

Mystical Experience

What is mystical experience? How many people have it, and how does it differ from just being religious?

Religious experience comes in many forms, in many types of dress. A Muslim or Hindu reaching a certain level of experience will describe it in different terms from a Christian reaching the same place. Each will not only describe it, but actually *see* it in terms of the imagery and concepts which are the currency of their religion. Underlying the different expressions, a common experience is recognizable, but you have to know what to look for. In other words, you have to understand the nature of the experience in neutral terms: the essence or principle of it.

Religious belief is the acceptance of some formal expression of deeper truths. Doctrines are communicated through words and images. However, direct experience is initially *wordless*. It is a feeling or sensation, a seeing or a hearing. The words, that is, the description or concept of it, follow from the attempt to integrate and make sense of the experience, to fit it in to your existing framework of ideas and beliefs. For a rough sort of image of the difference between what you believe and what you know from experience, you could say that concepts such as beliefs are things you know with and in your head, but that experience can strike you all over, including right in the viscera! You might feel deeply about a concept, but the sensations which arise with an experience are of a different order.

As to how widespread mystical experience is, it is unlikely that anyone who has tried to pursue religious life to any degree at all has not encountered some experiences of a powerful or significant nature, even if not all that often. There are probably many which pass unrecognized, for lack of knowing how to identify them, or because they did not seem particularly extraordinary, or because they are more of the nature of 'doings' or 'knowings' rather than some sudden wonderful experience arising apparently from outside oneself.

Different Kinds of Religious Experience

The examples given in the first chapter of 'moments out of time', moments of sudden peace or clarity, the feeling of having somehow changed gear, and of grasping significance, could be classified as a brush with meaning, just a fragile apprehension of meaningfulness. They do not happen frequently, but they are common to many if not all people. They may occur spontaneously without any religious intention, or as a result of setting up the conditions. The conditions could occur in a spiritual context, when praying for instance, or in an aesthetic one, when communing with nature or art, or could be physically based: trekking across deserts, scaling mountains and so forth.

Another category includes experiences of overwhelming feeling, perhaps a feeling of love, or protection, or awe, or worship. These feelings have a different intensity and quality from normal, and come, as it were, from somewhere else, unbidden, non-commandable, and seeming like a precious gift which you never quite forget although you may not be able to capture it again. Experiences like this will invariably be understood in terms of whatever image a person has of God or the divine, or the highest conceivable.

Religious experience is often identified with having visions: a vision of God, angels, deities or other holy apparitions. The image may be very real and detailed, and there is usually a message, a sense of something important being conveyed. The form of the image is placed upon it by the mind of the perceiver, but underlying this, in genuine experience, is a knowing of something, a meeting with something having real existence. Other visions are not concrete images, but are in the nature of insights: a vision of some truth. The hearing of sounds, or of a voice which communicates a religious meaning, is another type of experience in this category.

Seeing in images does not have to be a startling occurrence. It is a capacity which can be developed and utilized to further spiritual ends, and many people do so, without realizing that what they are doing is not so very different from what they have read about as occurring to the great exemplars of spirituality. Obviously, auditory and visual phenomena are open to misinterpretation and abuse. Genuine visionaries are unlikely to discuss their experience unless there is a reason to; and it serves to deepen their own understanding and insight rather than sending them off on some mission which involves persuading everybody else of the 'truth' of their vision or message. No formulated insight can ever be absolute truth, although it may seem so to the person who perceives it, and it may or may not have meaning for others. For oneself, the wisest course is not to set too much store on these phenomena, accepting what is helpful or meaningful in them, but not regarding them, or oneself, as particularly special for having encountered a little of the realities of religious life.

Nature and Supernature

The word 'supernatural' is misleading, meaning something above or more than nature, with the implication that such experiences are somehow not natural. If 'supernatural' is used to cover a whole range of non-ordinary experiences the question arises: how can anything occurring so universally, in every age, be any less than entirely natural to human beings, even if not as common as 'ordinary' experience? There are probably historical and cultural factors underlying the concept of supernatural, but it is certainly time for what is considered normal in human capacities to be measured from the greater as well as the lower extent of human experience.

Psychic or paranormal powers can be either inborn or developed. There is an immense amount of superstition surrounding them, just because most people are unaware of any capacity in themselves. Outside a religious context, such manifestations tend to be valued for their own sakes, and developed for a variety of purposes from healing to fortune-telling. Through meditation, some experience arises of the states which make possible phenomena such as telepathy, clairvoyance and astral travelling, but you may also see that there are states of being which are more important than these extraordinary ones. They are not particularly relevant to the aim of meditation, but for those interested in developing them there is literature available.

With all types of extra-normal experiences there are sometimes spontaneous manifestations, but they occur randomly, without much control, and they are either dismissed, not recognized, or turned to the sort of application which amounts to very little in real terms. The popular image of super-normal abilities is derived from exhibitions with curiosity value. However, what is the real point in foreseeing some national event like an earthquake or the death of a leader if there is nothing you can do about it anyway, and it has no relevance to your own behaviour? Likewise with any particular 'prediction', personal or otherwise, the question is: how useful is it? In the desire to know the future as it is commonly conceived, there is a large element of trying to avoid some disaster or to manipulate for personal gain, monetary or emotional. Fortunately, life is not so simple and open to manipulations from our baser motives like greed or fear! It may be possible to foresee events in this way, but how valuable a purpose does it serve?

However, it is possible to know the future in a way which is *meaningful* (see Chapter 9); but unless the capacity is recognized, and the mechanism for operating it understood, it is very difficult to trust it. Without trust, or 'the suspension of disbelief', experience cannot be increased. Forms of such experience are utilized by many people without being recognized as anything but some vague form of intuition, but with meditation they may become more familiar and conscious. The possibility of knowing the future or past, or prophecy, which is a form of profound insight, will be considered in the next chapter, because, properly, it is a development of the intellect.

Mythology and Symbolism

In all mythologies from every part of the world, detailed and fragmentary accounts of the meditative journey can be found. There are journeys through various celestial realms, or to the underworld; quests in search of a prize of great worth, such as the Holy Grail or Golden Fleece; pilgrimages to the Holy City; the traversing of courts, palaces and temples, or a series of valleys. All tree symbolism, spirals and mandalas, ladders and labyrinths are descriptions in different imagery of different levels of consciousness.

Some schools and philosophies of meditation describe altered states and the powers they open up in elaborate mythologies and imagery. The Eastern mythologies are the best-known. For example, there is the image of Kundalini, the serpent power coiled up at the base of the spine. It uncoils and rises as the Shakti, or female energy, to meet Shiva, the male energy, at the crown of the head, on the way opening up various centres which are described as lotuses or wheels, of various precise colours, petals or spokes, depending on the imagery.

The mythology can be further developed and made more concrete by personifying the powers of the centres as deities, which are encountered along the way. Their aspect, colour and the objects which they carry (in however many arms are needed to hold them) represent precisely the nature and qualities of the power, for those who recognize the experience. Books of the Dead are classic texts in this mode.

The disadvantage of this type of description is escalating superstition, not only from the 'uninitiated' to whom the experiences are not familiar and who interpret the imagery in all kinds of ways, literal or fanciful, but also from those 'treading the path', who see their experiences in terms of this imagery. Imagery which was appropriate and meaningful in other ages and in particular cultures does not reflect the psychological framework of this age, in this world culture. It contains information, and although it is not 'wrong', it may not be very helpful either.

Personification of experience in the form of gods, demons, or spiritual guides is obviously related very much to a certain culture, and people from a different background will not naturally see their own experience in terms of these figures. It is better to perceive the reality afresh, and the appropriate imagery will naturally arise. It will reflect your own background, which may well contain elements from what you have read, especially in an age in which information about the mythologies of many cultures is easily available. However, these will be elements which are meaningful for you.

For instance, in meditation you may become aware of activation on the top of the head. Some systems have characterized the feeling with the image of a thousand-petalled lotus. Your experience may be similar, or not, but if lotuses are not a feature of your regular environment, you may rather see it as a cabbage, or a rose. It is important not to be dazzled by the wealth of detail of mythologies which you do not wish to embrace as a totality, and not to expect to encounter experience in a particular form because such descriptions seem authoritative. An image may be accurate, but there is no 'right' way of perceiving the realities of experience. The important point is to be able to detach the essence of the experience from the imagery.

The Clothing of Experience in Imagery

Imagery is a sort of shorthand, a way of both preserving and communicating the kind of experience which falls outside the normal range. The associative mind naturally relates everything it encounters to a frame of reference which is familiar and concrete. An experience arises; in order to integrate and control it, the mind searches for the nearest equivalent with which it is familiar. For example, you may have an experience of effulgence, of light and power, of a creative source. What is the best concrete symbol to represent it, which will convey its qualities most succinctly and accurately if you wish to communicate it to someone else? In common with people of all cultures, you may instinctively choose the image of the sun. Solar imagery is universal, and although there are shades of difference between the meanings attributed to the sun in different cultures, the core or essence of the symbol can be understood by anyone on this planet.

Serpents figure widely in symbolism. There is no actual serpent coiled inside the body and rising up the spine, but you can become aware of a sensation for which this image is the nearest description. Similarly, during meditation you could feel wings. If your observation is clear, you may notice that the sensation accompanies a particular state. It is the state which is important; the sensation of wings is your mind attaching an image to the state, to characterize and maintain it, and through which it can be recognized on further occasions.

Not all experience is reducible to a single simple image, and there are many levels of meaning apart from the sensation aspect of the preceding examples. The mind may have to construct complex, abstract imagery to convey meaningful experience. It will build with known materials, images from the familiar world, but may end up with beings or events which have never graced the material earth! Composite mythical beasts are an example, as are heroic feats such as overcoming giants or monsters, or miraculous and bizarre possibilities like Jonah existing in the belly of a whale, or the argonauts navigating through clashing rocks. The symbolism can be read in various ways; it becomes meaningful when it can be related to one's own experience.

All symbolic description is clothing created by the mind. Although it is necessary for communication, there is also a trap if the clothing is mistaken for the reality and valued as the absolute and inviolate 'truth'. Wars are fought over these 'truths', and individual experience can be constrained and misdirected by not appreciating that descriptions are a limited and inadequate reflection of an area of experience which transcends the images. Anyone who develops the capacity to do so can apprehend the reality at first hand.

Meditative Experience

Meditation is a method for original apprehension. Only when the busy associating process of mental activity ceases to dominate, and allows the stillness and silence where meaning can be grasped, is it possible to enter simpler realms of experience. They are simpler because they are common and meaningful to all humanity, and closer to the creative source of experience itself.

True meditation demands the stripping away of imagery. When images arise, they are treated in the same way as all products of the mind: noted in passing beyond them, into the space from which they originate. When the observing consciousness does not attach itself to an image, despite the compelling emotional quality of imagery, this leads to the development of discrimination and detachment. Discrimination is the faculty for distinguishing between the appearances and the reality of any situation. Detachment is the ability not to be caught by any of the levels of clothing which conceal the heart of existence, and to continue perceiving more and further.

Meditation gives insight into almost all human states, some of which are accompanied by unusual powers. But in contrast to the disciplines which are aimed at awakening and developing extraordinary powers and abilities, in meditation such powers may be regarded as hindrances rather than confirmations of achievement. They should be treated like any other distraction tending to lead the meditator away from the central task. Some classic meditational literature is stern in its warnings against such seductive manifestations, because they are side-effects, not the essence of meditation. They are tools rather than aims, and are limited in scope compared with the infinite journey of meditation. If they are invested with great importance, they may become ends in themselves. Over the years a meditator will experience many remarkable things, but within the context of proper meditation training they will not necessarily have the emotional charge which they have for an untrained mind. By adherence to the instructions of meditation the meditator keeps them in perspective, and they do not upset psychological equilibrium. Inner doors open as the capacity to deal with the results matures.

Part of the training of meditation is in observation of inner states, because it is only by observing them that you are able to change them. Objective observation is based on the ability to distinguish the essential from the trappings (discrimination), and on being able to see without being drawn into or identified with the experience (detachment). Changes of state tend to happen in a sudden leap, a sort of quantum jump, or gear-change. However, they can be recognized by certain physical sensations which accompany them – changes in breathing, physical sensations in the head or other parts of the body, instant calmness. These electro-chemical effects in the body are useful as indicators. Meditators should be counselled simply to allow these sensations and pressures, without ascribing any importance to them, other than noting them as indications of a change of state, or of the gradual unlocking of potential changes of state when they recur over a period of time.

The Importance of Meditation

Meditation provides a structure and support for venturing into the unknown, and guidance to avoid being caught by the various psychological forces which inevitably arise to pull you back or off-course. It is not necessarily a long road to the Celestial City, but it is certainly fraught with obstacles!

There are forms of meditation in every religious tradition. All can lead through the same places, although in some forms it is easier than in others to get beyond the imagery to the essential ground upon which all are based. The background tradition does have an influence most of the way, but it progressively diminishes in its power to condition and control experience, as the meditator's acquaintance with the real essence of meditation is increased.

Because the knowledge it brings transcends imagery, meditation has no cultural boundaries. It does not promote division and differences. The language of meditational experience is understood by all who hear it with the ears of experience, no matter what their background, religious, racial, or perhaps even, planetary. It is unlikely that consciousness is confined to the planet Earth in view of the billions of planets in the universe. The essentials of consciousness will be the same, however vast the physical differences.

The diverse range of imagery to be found in classic religious texts from all over the world comes alive when the realities so described are recognizable to someone who has meditated for some time. Mythological stories are no longer charming fables, but contain information of relevance to anyone treading the inner path. A reputable meditation system provides both guide and map, drawing on the experience of all who have gone before. Without these one will almost inevitably go round in circles, or become bogged down in some way.

Meditation unifies through developing individual consciousness. We are at a stage in the life of humanity when national, cultural and religious boundaries are breaking down. Old structures of belief inevitably become encrusted with the bric-a-brac of centuries of self-interest and ideological self-preservation, and begin to lose power. When this happens, it is time for a reminder of the essentials on which traditions, especially religious traditions, are based. Meditation concentrates on the simplest of messages: the obligation to increase awareness and to *know* the divine. Therefore meditation acts as a force for unity in the world.

The power and primary function of a religion is not political or ethical jurisdiction over people's lives, but rather guiding spiritual life and preserving and teaching the methods of it. Any religion which loses sight of this, though it may continue to function as a social body and a channel for collective worship and aspiration, has lost the essential power of guiding individuals through to the deepest springs of religious knowledge. It is not through rationalizing dogma, but by returning to the roots of religious experience that it is possible to recognize the ground which is common to all religious humanity.

Deeper Human Experience and Authority

Traditionally, much of the experience outlined in this chapter has arisen in a religious context, orthodox or otherwise. In addition, there exists by now a very large body of religious/mystical texts which contain description and information. However, we are dealing with human experience, and it is not, and cannot be, restricted to a specifically religious approach. All such experience could be said to originate from the *base* of religion, the place from which all religions should take their authority, and where they genuinely meet. This base is accessible outside any conventional religious framework, and in the times we have reached, for many people this is the only acceptable option. A discipline like meditation offers a method of achieving deeper human experience outside existing religious frameworks.

However, some provision must be made for checking and containing such tendencies as self-aggrandizement, the pre-occupation with or abuse of power, and self-motivated claims to authority. With deeper experience of the power of consciousness, the self-oriented tendencies which are in all of us can get out of hand. To date, the checks on meditation were provided by a religious background and structure. When this no longer operates, meditation must be conducted under the guidance of a good instructor and within a context of personal discipline. Religion lends a framework for sorting out a hierarchy of values and a code of morality, and these are a necessary part of the process of growing, with or without religion. In fact, meditation without morality can be dangerous, like opening Pandora's box. The balance between meditation and living, between the needs and motivations of one's personality and the demands of inner growth, has to be maintained, or meditation is a self-indulgence. There will be results, but not of a very high order.

Meditation without checking and proper guidance introduces elements not only of danger, but of futility and self-defeat. It is a waste to attempt a course of action with far-reaching consequences without giving yourself the chance, not only of keeping to it (difficult on your own), but of attaining the full possibilities and benefits of a method designed to unlock a treasure-house of human experience which is greater than personal. Meditation is not a solo enterprise. Individual freedom and initiative do not mean 'going it alone', at the expense of accepting authoritative guidance.

True individuality gives the power to make decisions and hold values which owe nothing to fashion but come from an inner strength and balance which cannot be bought, nor swallowed in one easily-digested capsule. Times *have* changed. Nowadays, no-one in the West need be compelled by social pressures to conform to any particular *religious* orthodoxy. However, there exists a powerful *social* orthodoxy, a climate of distrust of any authority, including your own. Being able to distinguish what is genuine from that which is merely claimed, or is rather shallow, and yet being able to submit to the authority of others in a particular area until you have gained the experience yourself is the way to develop your own authority. Pervasive social doctrines and attitudes constitute as cramping a mental framework as any formerly religious ones.

In the end, genuine individuality is a capacity for trust, intelligent trust, and respect for human nature, the sort of respect which has become very unfashionable in an insecure climate of fear, meaninglessness, and pragmatism. A view of human beings as 'the most destructive animal on earth', which compares humanity unfavourably with peaceful gorilla groups playfully grooming their young in a leafy jungle hideaway, perpetuates a highly unconstructive indulgence in self-loathing. What is missing in our contemporary self-image is a sense of scale, and a realistic recognition of the power and scope of human potential when it is directed towards acknowledging and actualizing the divine dimension in all creation.

Chapter 9

The Creative Intellect

The sort of experience we have been discussing in the last chapter is very potent, but there is still further to go in the meditative journey. Powerful experiences alter your emotional foundation, changing your values and view of what is really meaningful, and you grow as a result of this internal reorganization. There comes a stage, however, when the *personal* benefits you may derive from meditation, such as peace, stability, power, or whatever it is which makes meditation very important to you, are no longer relevant as motivations. You glimpse something about meditation which makes continuing to meditate worthwhile *for its own sake*.

What motivates anyone normally is personal benefit, whether working for a living, going to a party, or practising meditation. You do it because you hope to get something out of it. In the earlier stages of meditation the mind lays greatest importance on those experiences which are personally meaningful, that is, those with an emotional charge. Other experiences are forgotten or missed because they do not seem directly relevant to you and your life now, or do not move you emotionally. There may come a stage in meditation when all the interesting experiences of your extending awareness seem to stop. If you can relate only to what is *personally* meaningful, you will have reached your limits. However, by now, you know that there is more. You will have had glimpses of the scope of meditation, and to proceed further you have to invest emotional energy into this larger sphere so that it becomes more meaningful, even though the meaning is not personal.

Acting without the motive of personal gain is a considerable jump. The paradox of this development is that there *are* personal benefits, but only when you stop looking for them. If there are no obvious benefits for the individual at this stage of meditation, why should anyone bother to put in the effort to continue? Part of the motivation comes from insight into the nature of the reality which underlies meditation, and from tasting the wider worlds of experience which are possible. In addition, there is a drive in human beings which is very important: the drive to do what can be done, simply because it is possible.

Curiosity and the Drive to Extend Experience

In all fields of activity people engage in dangerous, difficult or apparently pointless endeavours with the justification: 'because it's there', or 'why not?' Far from being absurd, this reflects a fundamental impulse in human beings. It is, in fact, a highly abstract motivation, in the sense of being without immediate personal benefit except that which comes from the satisfaction of confronting a challenge. The challenge may be both personal and, as it were, on behalf of humanity: Man versus the Environment. Often there is considerable danger in terms of personal survival. Scientific discoveries and research of all kinds can be traced to the same basic drive to confront the challenge of the unknown and extend the boundaries of the possible.

Without an inherent, unquenchable curiosity to know more, we would probably still be living in caves, or in the trees, or already be extinct. Indeed, it is impossible to conceive of human nature minus this curiosity. We are distinguished from the rest of animal life on earth by questioning, by seeking always to go beyond the necessities of survival, to refine and perfect the methods of achieving anything, to push into any territory which is unknown or not yet mastered.

Some might be tempted to think that curiosity can outstrip good sense. Often it does, because creative enterprises are more often motivated by sheer curiosity than by concern about how ideas can be applied. However, good sense catches up one way or another because we have to live with the practical results of our ideas. Ultimately, history records the final verdict on the usefulness of ideas or inventions. Those which are of use are meaningful, and these are retained and developed. The rest are discarded. What is meaningful for the race might not be the same as that which is considered so by individuals. You might feel, for example, that the preservation of the planet in a particular state which is important to you is of more value than the continual out-reaching impulse which operates without aiming at obvious practical benefits, or apparently at the expense of needs which are extremely obvious. Were you able to implement this judgement, you would be demanding that curiosity be confined to the service of the ends *you* have identified as meaningful.

Unfortunately, or fortunately, curiosity is not pragmatic. It seeks to know for its own sake, and if ever that impulse ceased, so too would human life. The capacity for abstract motivation, for pursuing principles without looking for personal or immediate rewards, is part of our survival mechanism, the survival not only of the physical life we share with other species, but of the psychological life which is uniquely human.

Meditation is the greatest of all challenges, especially when a meditator reaches 'the dark night of the soul' (St John of the Cross), the stage when personal rewards seem to dry up, and the character of the urge to meditate changes to a more abstract awareness of the worth of meditating for its own sake. However, from this point onwards, meditation becomes truly creative.

Creativity and Consciousness

There are always practical spin-offs from abstract enterprises like pure research, but they are often unforeseen, in unexpected and new directions. Anything which can be foreseen is associative, the result of some logical progression of thought or development. The hallmark of the genuinely creative is that it arises of itself, either unexpectedly or in ways of which the details cannot be completely predicted. In meditation, beyond a certain point, you might not *see* any concrete, practical benefit to yourself as an individual. It is then that meditation touches upon true creativity.

The physical creativity of procreation is one form of our deeply implanted drive towards the creative. This and all creative enterprises are motivated in the same way – unconsciously. All the reasons and rationalizations which can be mustered to support any 'because-it's-there' activity are attempts of the conscious mind to justify and integrate the impulse, because no one explanation or justification is ever sufficient on its own, and counter-arguments can almost always be produced. For example, there are many arguments against enterprises like the thrust into space, mostly pragmatic and to do with the cost and the military usage of the technology. However, the drive towards the conquest of space, terrestrial or extra-terrestrial, is evidently present in the human species as a whole, and always has been. The chances of quashing it in the long term are infinitesimal. It is a motivation which is neither rational nor conscious.

All the less pragmatic drives in human beings – towards beauty, art, delight for its own sake, or knowledge – are unconscious and as primitive and essential for us as those drives we have in common with other species of life on earth. They are not some evolutionary embellishment, nor a flight of fancy with little evolutionary value. For example, the universal urge to decorate, evident from the earliest pots and artifacts, has no physical survival value, but there is obviously some essential and enduring impulse towards making utilitarian objects more beautiful, which is important for our psychological life.

Meditation is a means for fulfilling the urge to extend knowledge of human nature, the internal universe as well as the external, and needs no further justification. It begins to unlock an area which was previously unconscious, giving access to a buried reserve of potential by bringing it into conscious awareness, and enabling conscious command of it. The power of original thought – the power to bring the new into the world and give it form, whether in art, or words, or scientific conception and discovery – is developed through meditation, and becomes less dependent on fortuitous circumstance and external conditions. The channel for the creative is the intellect.

The Intellect

It is quite difficult to talk about the intellect, because 'intellectual' has various connotations relating to cleverness, or ivory-tower manipulations of abstruse concepts, or head-dominated remoteness from concrete feelings and sensuality. The reason that a large proportion of the human race would not dare admit to having an 'intellect' at all is that genuine intellect is so little understood. The idea that it may be a tool for dealing with the world, a faculty to receive information and process it for purposes as practical as the organization of living, is obscured by the way it is identified with academic pursuits. Equally, the idea that the intellectual capacity, which every normal human being has, can be developed and greatly extended in a way which has nothing at all to do with 'brainy-ness' is generally an unfamiliar one.

You do not need 'brains', in the popular sense, to live an integrated and meaningful life, and you do not need them to be wise. What is wisdom, but a capacity for insight into the meaning of events, and the ability to act upon it? Not everyone may have the inclination towards academic learning, but it is a common birthright, no matter how good or bad our memory for facts or ability to handle abstract reasoning, to be able to increase understanding and wisdom if we should choose to do so. Not everyone does choose to, of course; in fact, very few are prepared for the self-discipline which it demands.

The intellect is properly understood as an integral function of every human being, not some specialized skill or innate talent. Everyone interacts with the external world in three ways: through acting upon it, by feeling about it, and by ordering it through some sort of reasoning or thinking process. The last is the area of the intellect. Obviously, people differ in their command of it, just as some are more physically agile than others, or more emotionally vulnerable than others. Just as bodily skills and feeling reactions can be commanded and worked upon, so the intellect can be developed, both in depth and in dexterity or 'muscle'.

However, thinking itself is not the intellect, but rather one of its operations. Thinking is always associative, relating ideas according to some logical progression, ordering and classifying them perhaps into new or more useful groups, but always with a basis in already familiar concepts and associated to familiar conscious experience. It is a particular skill, and it can also be developed with practice. Academic philosophy, for example, is of this nature, along with 'intellectual' or academic thought in general.

Intellect is a wider function, encompassing more than a logical process for sorting out data. Intellect is an organ for receiving impressions and information. It classifies and relates all the impressions which enter in the course of living, but not necessarily according to the rules of logic or rationality. There are other criteria for classifying experience, such as by reference to their personal meaning.

The intellect has an emotional foundation, and the more the intellectual function is developed and extended, the more relevant is the role of meaning as an organizing factor. Greater emotional clarity produces more intellectual power. When thinking touches upon meaning, there is a change of quality. The dimension of meaning brings in emotional power. It is then less easy to get lost in mazes of elaborate conceptual structures which are logically consistent, but meaningless in terms of grasping life. Thinking with a concern for meaning brings in depth and power, and creativity.

However, working from an emotional foundation is not the same as identifying personally with an issue. When you take something *personally*, you become vulnerable, and your objectivity is clouded by feelings, desires, preferences, insecurities and so forth, which are nothing to do with real intellect. The characteristic of intellect is objectivity, but objectivity does not mean lack of involvement such as that which can lead to the meaninglessness of sophisticated associative thinking. Objectivity is a capacity to see in a larger context all the time. The root of this capacity is a grasp of meaning. The intellect is a sensory organ, a thinking mechanism, and a catalyst for transforming experience through the creative perception which is insight.

Insight

Much of the truly original thought which makes its mark in setting a new direction in any field, or underlies art which endures, results from insight. Insight is usually sudden, a perception or conception which seems to 'come out of the blue', often when least expected, as in the famous Archimedes instance, and in scientific serendipity. Invariably, though, there has been a great deal of work previous to the break-through. The relevant facts need to be consciously mustered and worked through by the normal process of mental slog: associative reasoning. To allow the sudden gelling, the creative leap, it seems necessary to disengage this process, however, by turning one's attention to something else, like taking a bath or a walk, or anything which dislodges conscious concentration and allows a 'gap' of relative internal quiet through which something of another order can enter. The more intensely consciousness has been occupied with the problem, perhaps to the point of being wearied out of its normal competent functioning, the more likely it is that when it ceases to try there will be a sort of temporary vacuum of internal silence, which is exactly what allows the results of unconscious functioning through into consciousness.

When the mind is totally engaged on some problem, there is a sorting out and synthesizing taking place unconsciously. The mechanism in this situation is the same as that which meditation utilizes. Restricted to a specific issue, like solving a problem, the unconscious activity may cause a solution to appear suddenly in consciousness. Some people learn how to set up the conditions favourable to spontaneous insight, and the resulting 'inspiration' is the power upon which art and every form of creative endeavour depend. Meditation is regular practice in setting up conditions for the intellect to work creatively in this way, but not only when applied to an individual project. Through meditation your thinking and outlook on everything are affected.

Meditation establishes the prerequisites for using the power of unconscious processes, which work on different principles from conscious thinking, and on a different time-scale. Unconscious in everyone is potential experience which remains formless until it is brought into consciousness. Becoming aware of more extended experience and putting form upon it, through articulating or acting upon it, is genuinely creative. Something entirely new is brought into existence. There is no limit to the application of insight. It will transform your life and perception.

Time and the Unconscious

Mulling over a problem and having the solution pop suddenly

into your head when you do not expect it is a fairly common experience. But why should laborious and persistent *logical* thinking not produce the answer eventually? How is it that you may seem to be banging your head against a wall, until sometimes months or even years later the way forward, or missing piece, suddenly becomes evident? The solution appears instantaneous. It bears no obvious correlation to the amount of time you may have put in. Once it has appeared, you set about formulating it by normal conscious thinking.

Time in the unconscious is not the same as that of consciousness. Time as we normally perceive it is a conscious ordering, a set of sequential units of 'presentness', combined into bigger groupings of minutes, days, weeks, etc. It is a logical ordering. Unconscious processes transcend these divisions of time, which are a construct needed for arranging ordinary living. Ideas can be formulated unconsciously, connections being made without your being aware of anything happening. You notice only when the synthesis springs into consciousness.

The perception of conscious time is variable. Perception does not always correspond to the time marked by the clock. The most common examples occur in crisis events such as an impending car accident: in the moment when the inevitability of a collision is evident, time seems to slow dramatically. People usually describe it as 'everything went into slow motion'. When this happens, every detail of the disaster can be recalled later, because there seemed to be plenty of time, with observation concentrated to a razor-sharp degree by the presence of death. Other dramatic events jolt us out of our normal time-perception, like the moment of shock in receiving bad news. There is a phenomenon which occurs when facing death such as by drowning, when time does a fast rewind, and one's whole life passes before one's eyes in an instant.

Less dramatic emotional states also influence the way time is perceived or felt. In love, and waiting for a rendez-vous with the beloved, we experience even short spaces of time as immensely long, whereas when the meeting is achieved, time just seems to fly! There is nothing like boredom for causing time to creep on leaden feet, and nothing like consuming interest for moving it along too fast.

Events which are in the past, and long-gone as far as our conscious memory is concerned, may still be very much present as a motivating force on an unconscious level. Or they may suddenly surface as the fruition or confirming factor of a long-term process which they appear almost to have brought about. Something happens, and immediately a lot of memories and connections arise, and it may seem that 'this is the moment you have been waiting for'.

Creative Thought

Genuinely creative thought is independent of time as it is normally perceived. It could be said that the skill of creative thinking is actually allowing the unconscious to work as it can. You have to collect in your mind all the relevant information, but you must be prepared to wait with patience for new internal connections to be made. Unconscious processes take time, and understanding will emerge into consciousness when the organization is complete. Then it can be worked with consciously and organized further. With more experience in meditation you begin to trust unconscious processes more, because the nature of meditation demands trust. As you do so, the processes become more recognizable. Two types of thought can be identified.

One feels like a long, slow turning-over, like a huge slow wheel. You are aware of 'things going on' within, of changes taking place, of pushes and pulls, but you cannot say exactly what they are or where they are leading. This aspect in meditation is the repeated effort you put into it, and the sense of changing within yourself. With regard to thinking, it can be felt when there is something you need to understand. You keep returning to it, and it may be a little clearer, or you may sense new meanings which you cannot fully grasp. This may continue for weeks or even years. You can actually feel it carrying on while you do everything else, until one day, just as the continued push of a mushroom breaks through concrete, you know what you need to know. With continued meditation, one day you find that you have changed; you realize that you are not reacting in the same way to something as you would have, say, a year ago. You are, in fact, new.

The other thought process could be described as gestative. It is a brooding and hatching which occurs in darkness, not so much a repeated input with unnameable changes as a steady growth occurring in some place where you cannot poke at it. The result emerges fully formed, as it were. This is the mechanism, for example, behind tucking an idea away in the back of your mind and leaving it there, waiting till it reappears with all the necessary connections, no longer the partly formed 'germ' of an idea, but fully-fledged and operational.

These two modes of thought work together creatively to synthesize meaning, to bring what is genuinely new into the world. No linking together of associations has a fraction of the scope and power of this process. It is powerful because what arises from it brings about changes in people and ideology. Change occurs because, quite simply, such insights are *useful*, and provide an explanation or foundation for a whole lot more. All great break-throughs, the leaps which individuals, groups or humanity itself have made, have originated from insight, or creative vision, or non-derivative, non-associative thought. Break-throughs of this kind happen of course without a training like meditation, but meditation works upon the intellect to develop its creative possibilities in a systematic fashion.

The Transcending of Time

Another consequence of the development of real intellect, and of recognizing and trusting processes which are unconscious, manifests itself in the ability to know forwards and backwards from the conscious time we ordinarily inhabit. This was referred to in the previous chapter in the context of paranormal powers, and a distinction was made between fairly random glimpses of events in the future and a meaningful 'seeing'.

Seeing the solution to a problem is almost like receiving a vision of it already existing in the future. Some people describe their insights this way, as if the reality exists somewhere, in some other time-frame. Once you have looked 'ahead' and seen it, you can then interpret it into ideas, and set to work bringing it about in the physical world. Some time later, there it is, maybe not exactly as you have foreseen it in detail, but in essence the same. The details are not important. In fact, the more detail you try to foresee, the more likely it is that your prediction will not tie up with the actuality. All the forces which come into play to shape and concretize a conception will develop it according to their own logic.

Seeing the future is, in part, a question of being able to read the logic of situations. It is not only a mysterious apprehension of the essence or meaning of what will eventuate; it is also a result of clear observation of what is, now, not distorted or directed by personal interest; a result of viewing all possibilities with an equal eye and allowing them to be what they are. The seeds of the future are all in the present. Non-attached reading of present facts (as opposed to interpretations of the facts) is the key, because the logic of them and how they will develop is then apparent. It is, of course, very difficult to see the present. The lenses through which normally we look are compounded of personal feelings and reactions. Only when these lenses are quite worn away, and there is true non-attachment, is the art of seeing really mastered. Meditation works upon the lenses, extending the boundaries of our meaningful universe.

Many people, however, know what is meant by seeing into the future in this way, and have had some experience of it, although they may not have articulated it, or thought much about it. It is only when you make it conscious, and are aware of what you are doing, that you can utilize the ability. A not uncommon example is knowing the nature and sex of an unborn child. Particularly for a mother, the new life is part of her own life and flesh; this kind of knowledge about such a significant event is highly relevant in ways more important than knowing what colour to paint the room. Knowing a child before its birth is different in nature from guessing or wishful thinking. It is characterized by a quality of certainty and clarity, but women who feel this way will probably keep quiet about it, instinctively, for sound reasons.

Another example of seeing into the future could be when you have strong feelings or some intuition about a certain place the minute you arrive, a sense that it is important for you, although you have never been there or had any connection with the place before. Later this is proved correct because you make your home there, or your career, or meet the love of your life there, or some event connected with the place changes your life. What is going on? It could be said that what you sensed initially was an apprehension of the future, that some part of you knew what the situation would be five years on. This way of looking at the phenomenon is a means of interpreting a perception which is quite real – if you give it credence and pay attention to it. If you do not, the perception remains dim and slips away. Your *consciousness* must attach to something if you are to perceive it. In this fashion we control perception, by what we recognize and are prepared to accept as meaningful; and this is why some people perceive what others do not.

The more conscious you become of events which transcend time, the more aware you will be of their occurring. Or, in other words, the more they will occur. You make your reality. It is important to trust the experience which your intellect assesses as genuine insight into the nature of the real world, especially when there is little support from others whose reality excludes the possibilities you are aware of yourself. Disbelief is catching, because it is far less demanding than the effort of extending your consciousness to encompass a bigger view of reality. Belief is not much use either, for 'accepting things on the hearsay of others' does not increase experience. Trust is really a matter of suspending disbelief, until you are in a position to know, from incontrovertible experience and visible manifestation, whether something is so or not. However, there is no point in trying to convince others; they will either believe or disbelieve, until they, too, know from experience.

Handling knowledge of the future needs a very light touch, or it will descend from meaningful to banal, or quite simply, wrong. The rules of the art demand that it not be used for personal gain, and personal gain may be the motivation for talking about it, with an unconscious intention of increasing your esteem in the eyes of others. Experience will soon show that if you announce your 'predictions' when there is no need, or try to see all kinds of details out of mere curiosity, or delight in a feeling of power or control over the future or over others, you will be caught out, because the details will unfold differently. Only what is meaningful is genuinely forseeable, that is, meaningful for you to base your conduct upon in the present, so that it leads to the *realization* of what you have foreseen in its essential form. Meaningless detail is likely to be wishful thinking, and because it is meaningless, your actions will not bring it about.

This raises the question: are you getting a preview of a future which already exists in the sense of being already determined, and which simply unfolds fairly inevitably, or is your seeing of it more accurately a *conceiving*, which in some sense actually creates the future? The latter introduces the element of will, will which is a creative force, of the same nature as the intellectual capacities we have been discussing. The predetermined view is simplistic, based on the notion that linear conscious time is the extent of reality.

Seeing into the past is in some ways easier than knowing ahead. This chapter has explored seeing the future because this illustrates the principles of visionary ability, and its relevance to the growth of being. The key to all such powers is meaningfulness, because they originate in a dimension where time does not function as we know it consciously. In its place is a structure created by the interconnectedness of meaning. If something which occurred in the far past has meaning for you, then it is possible for you to make real contact with that meaning and the events which embodied it, because the *meaning* is still existent. Meaning itself cannot be 'past'; it is related to your perception.

Into the Silence

Through the intellect, experience is ordered, and the world of your perception established. The intention of this chapter has been to illustrate how that world can be extended. Some capacities which result from developing the intellect have been explored at length, although not exhaustively, in order to establish a few guidelines for understanding the principles by which they work. It is important to recognize that these faculties are part of our human heritage, not some weird excursion into fantastical, super-human abilities.

Above all, meditation orders experience, both ordinary experience and the less common, and from this ordering into meaningful patterns, a foundation is established which allows experience to be extended. If you are totally preoccupied trying to cope with a life of emotional chaos and moral vacuum, you will have no time or energy left to notice, let alone explore and increase that awareness which is based on simplicity and wholeness.

The territory which opens up as a result of meditation is new and unknown, but gradually it becomes organized. It is not that the sort of experiences we are talking about can be achieved only by meditation, but meditation enables you to understand them, so that they can be fully integrated without your being overwhelmed by them, as sometimes happens during so-called 'mystical experience'. Normally, the doors to the unknown remain closed. Meditation opens them little by little, revealing the path of knowledge beyond, and enables you to proceed along it step by step. It is a path into silence, the primeval potent silence in which worlds may come into being.

Chapter 10

Silence

The true intellect at work, and the area of knowledge it opens up, can be recognized by an obvious characteristic: the mind becomes silent. In ordinary life, there are rare times when the mind stills, and dwells in a sort of void. The difference between this and the normal babble of associations and internal conversations is almost shocking, and normally the stillness cannot be held once you become aware of it. The mind immediately starts up its commentary, because it naturally abhors a vacuum.

However, it is within this apparent 'void' that real, creative thought can occur. Meditation promotes and trains the capacity for silent potency. Through your will, which is not desire, and not wilfulness, the mind empties of its mechanical thoughts and daydreams, and if at this point consciousness is steady and the state maintained, then the silence will be filled, as it were 'from above', rather than 'from below' with mental chatter. The first stage is creative thought. Every stage or level beyond this occurs in deeper and deeper silence.

In this chapter we go further into it, beyond meaning with its personal relevance, beyond even the long, slow processes of creative thought, to later stages of consciousness still attached to a sense of identity. You are conscious of yourself, and you are conscious of something greater, which you may call the Divine, or God, or the Numinous, or Knowledge. What you call it, and the sort of concept which you find most satisfying as a description, will reflect a very deep predisposition within your nature, the motivation which has led you to this point. People's base-level motivations differ; hence they will have different ways of describing what they find at this stage when their motivation encounters a reality which satisfies it. These differences can account for the most basic conflicts dividing humanity.

It is vital to recognize that the reality itself is not the same as, and cannot be contained by, any descriptions given to it. There is this God, and that God, and the other God, and all of them, if they can be conceived of and characterized by words or images, are descriptions by some one or some many, reflecting what he, she or they are able to comprehend of a vastness which is not captured by any of them.

Motivations

The many different ways in which people characterize the divine or greater reality can be divided into three fundamental approaches. These approaches can be recognized in individuals, cultures and religions.

Some are drawn towards and seeking the Light, and all it represents psychologically. In this line are all expressions of the need to worship, to celebrate the glory of God and the divine, to seek an effulgence before which one can kneel. It is a longing which is directed towards radiance and power, or en*light*enment.

Some search out the Dark, the darkness of beginnings, of origins, of the source of manifestations. This is an expression of the need to know, to trace things back to their roots and source. It means probing into the darkness, which veils the origins of all things, and into the mystery of power and of God within. It is a line of knowledge.

Some seek Communion, to relate to and ultimately become one with the Highest. This urge underlies the lover and beloved relationship, the desire for union, for self-immolation, and the impulse to sacrifice in all its forms.

As with all psychological classifications, the categories are not mutually exclusive. All three are present in everybody, to some degree, and strands of each can be recognized in all religions. However, the more one moves towards simplicity, towards identifying the primary strands which make up the complex tapestry of any identity, the clearer the basic elements or predispositions become. The underlying motivation is what gives any entity its 'flavour', its character, and determines what is emphasized. If everything received equal emphasis, there would be no differentiation between people, and between their ideological sympathies. But clearly there are enormous differences.

The understanding that there may be an underlying bias in motivation, which is so deep and unconscious that it is not recognized, explains a great deal of the bitterness and fervour in the conflicts which originate in areas which are most important to people. Above all, in the approach to the divine, what people seek in order to meet their underlying need or aspiration, they will find – and that will be the nature of God to them. The approach conditions the aspects of reality which are recognized, and the description given to it. Reality itself cannot be encompassed by any description.

Gods

It may be worth looking more closely at the nature of aspiration. It could be said that the concept of 'God' defines what a person sees as the Highest. If your job, for example, is the most important thing for you, without which life becomes effectively meaningless, then it is in reality your 'god'. You may believe in a Divine Being as defined by your religious adherence, but if it came to a crunch, and you had to choose between them, the one which was more important to you would represent your real aspiration and establish where you wished to put your energy. Lip-service, duty or convention are not the hallmarks of aspiration, which is actually a shaping force, powerful in its long-term effects.

Looked at this way, an apparently 'godless society' may actually be full of gods; but the problem is that they are very small, commanding aspirations which are limited, and extremely fragile. If work, family, pleasure, artistic achievement, or wealth represent your highest aim and aspiration, you set them up as your gods, and what happens when you lose them? You either go to pieces, or look for a larger definition of the greatest to which you can aspire, and use that to pull your life together. The wider and more encompassing the aspiration you identify in yourself, the more use it is in coping with change, or suffering.

You set up as god what you see as the highest, either consciously or unconsciously; and whether or not you achieve the aspiration, it sets the upper limit of your possible achievement. The higher your aspiration, the more you can develop towards it. Aspiration is always more than what you are, but it pulls up what you are.

What you see as the upper limit is a very important question when it comes to meditation, because it determines how far you can go. If you have a limited view of where meditation can take you, you will never get beyond it. In an open-ended enterprise like meditation, any image will act as a limitation, no matter how elevated. It will restrict your possibilities to the ones you are able to conceive of. Therefore, to be in a position to realize or know the fullness of meditation, your conception of God, or the Divine, or Enlightenment, needs to be beyond images. For example, it is possible to be aware of a vast order which cannot be comprehended ordinarily. If you can trust in that, it can serve as an aiming-point, and it is a big enough frame of reference to use for something like meditation.

What a person sets up as the highest depends on his or her essential type. As an illustration of how responses can differ in emphasis, take three people entering a wood on a summer's day. One may be most delighted by all the beauties to be found there, the sun filtering through the trees, small flowers in the grass, the song of birds, and will search out one after another to admire, in an almost worshipful spirit. Another, sensing the beauty of the place, will primarily want to sit in stillness and commune with the spirit of the wood, as it were, or feel at one with it. The third wants also to understand the essence of the experience, to pursue questions like the nature of beauty or 'treeness' as far as they may lead. For this person, awareness of beauty is not so much a revelation of the wonder of creation, or a state to be enjoyed, but a stimulus for seeking knowledge of the whys and wherefores of created existence.

The first illustrates the Light aspect, the second the impulse towards Communion, and the third the desire to know causes, or to probe the Dark. In reality, all these impulses will probably be intermingled in a person's response. The primary drive can be distinguished, however, and sometimes it is possible to recognize that it is predominating in the way a particular situation is approached. Not only does the form of religious experience reflect what an individual desires to find as ultimate meaning but also religions themselves embody a bias in their basic philosophy or approach.

In almost all traditions of religion or mythology, there are trinities, groups of three which illustrate three related aspects of a concept. This makes a point about the importance of threeness for human beings. Any proper totality has three aspects. One should be wary of trying to interpret one trinity with reference to another, however. Mythologies are complex. Threeness occurs at different psychological levels. For example, the Christian trinity does not express the same concept as Brahma, Vishnu, Shiva, and embodies a different perspective on the divine. Briefly, one way of identifying the three principles is to say that there is one which initiates or is active, one which receives or embodies, and one which infuses or holds the balance. Or one affirms, one denies, and one unifies. The latter formulation is reflected in the three types of motivation. One is basically affirming creation and the power within it, one denies the illusion of it and looks to the origins or causes, and one balances the changes in order to maintain the unity of creation.

Meditation and Truth

A person's individual motivation or innate perspective will condition the way in which God is seen, whether in aspiration or realization. There is an inherent danger, which is at the root of much misunderstanding and conflict. The problem is that this 'seeing' inevitably appears to be the truth, the only right way of seeing the divine, the only way it can truly be known. For the perceiver, it *is* God, it is indeed the highest perception of reality, worth living for, fighting for, dying for. If God is primarily Love for you, if entering into a personal relationship with God and seeking oneness is of paramount importance and meaning, those religions or individuals who see God as a remote, law-giving Father, or who seek to enquire into the workings of things and value knowledge more than worship, not only may, but will almost seem either wrong or of lesser importance and truth.

Such is the nature of fundamental leanings, and especially of perception. The danger can even be exacerbated by meditation, because reality is encountered according to your preconditioning. It is a matter no longer of ideas and beliefs, but of personal experience, so your own viewpoint and perception appear to be re-inforced. Therefore it is absolutely vital to understand the process by which deeper experience is clothed, and to accept that there may be different motivations, simplified into three primary drives, and to recognize that *there is always more*. Meditation will ultimately take you to the source of motivation, where there will arise an understanding and some experience of all three kinds.

The stage when some very fundamental (to you) meaning is grasped, or revelation arises, is not the end of the journey. At the stage we are concerned with in this chapter, meditation confronts the meditator with his or her own motivation. Many, having persevered, and extended themselves to this point, stop extending when they encounter truths or insights of this nature and at this level, for they have found what they were looking for. Revelations at this stage, accompanied by considerable personal power and the conviction born of experience – and uncommon experience at that, are sufficient to begin a new religion, or sect, or movement, if a person feels that the truth he or she has perceived should be promulgated.

In the Prelude to this book, meditation was compared with a voyage. The stage of the journey we are dealing with here is the point when something profound is achieved. All the previous major stopping-off points have been passed, even though there are revelations of all degrees arising throughout the journey, and it is possible to take any of them as the truth. By this stage, there is a simplicity and therefore power, which is even more beguiling. It is represented in the Prelude as finding oneself alone in a small but sturdy boat (though one may have set off in quite an elaborate or stately vessel), and finally within reach of the goal of one's predilection. It could be the star which symbolizes one's deepest longing, a source of illumination commanding worship; or the darkness of space with its possibilities for knowledge of untold worlds and systems; or the realization that the star and the darkness and oneself are all part of a wondrous reality, and that merging oneself with them in journeying is fulfilment.

However, especially as there is still divergence in what is recognized as most meaningful, this cannot be the ultimate face of reality. One has to leave the boat. The image of a boat stands for meditation itself, the means of journeying, the method which has brought one to confront the deepest aspect of oneself as an individual identity. Leaving the boat amounts to a leap into the unknown. The journey is not a continuous progression towards an aim which could be conceived of, however fragmentarily, at the outset, but involves now a quantum jump into a dimension which is new. Meditation, at some stage, has to be left behind.

The Temple Within

Meditation is not only a practice to be done at specific times in the day: it becomes a way of life, affecting every facet of your personal reality. You may not have been meditating for very long before the process can be felt continuing outside designated sessions, whenever the attention is turned to the place of meditation inside yourself. Once the sound or object of meditation is embedded in the psyche, it is always there. It is to assist the implantation of it that the initiation, when a meditator is given his or her meditational focus, should be formal or in some way made significant. This first step towards creating a temple within clears a psychological space, which is easier to return to if it has been demarcated clearly, and given some sort of emotional boost by special conditions.

With continued meditation the place becomes more and more familiar, stronger and more potent, a point of balance and a source of strength in handling the challenges of daily life, which can be as demanding and mundane as trying to deal with three urgent things at once when you have a cold and are pressured by lack of time! If you know the place of meditation, go there and act from it.

The importance of the meditation object is functional. Behind it, so to speak, is silence. During a session the sound or image sometimes fades into this silence, and you follow it there – which is not the same as losing attention or going off into daydreams.

The silence is the same as that in which the processes of creative thought take place. It is the silence which characterizes all excursions into the higher functions, however brief. It is recognizable not only by the absence of the chattering mind and its continual commentary, but by a potency which is both empty and full at the same time. It is unmistakable when it is known. There is no question of the mind going 'blank', with all that this phrase conjures up in the way of vacancy, voidness and sheer impossibility. The silence is rich; it is very much alive, almost vibrant, and although there is no-thing which can be grasped, there is a sense of fullness.

This level of silence exists within everything; it is a level of simplicity underlying the complexity, which can be reached at any time if you are familiar with it. There is silence in you all the time, even *while* your mind is babbling, and part of the skill lies in trusting it. As you trust it, you begin to feel it. It becomes a conscious reality for you.

Quietism

There is a danger in going after silence as a goal in itself: the danger of 'quietism'. Silence, quiet, a tranquil mind are extremely pleasant. If states of silence and quiet are valued for themselves, there is a tendency to seek to avoid conflict or anything which may disturb one's tranquillity. It may mean repudiating rather than dealing with a lot of the negatives like anger and aggression. It leads ultimately to passivity, in which action is valued less than sitting and contemplating with a quiet mind, and to the belief that this is the best possible state for human beings to be in. Ordinary life can seem unimportant compared with entering into silence and communing with whatever is found there, call it the Divine or Reality or what you will.

The attitude is often promoted in books about meditation, where the world is treated as irrelevant and a hindrance to the enjoyment of higher states, while the image of someone sitting motionless in continual meditation appears to be the goal we should all aspire to as the highest manifestation of the art, as if doing nothing were its finest fruit. It is a serious temptation, because there is a great deal of enjoyment, peace and satisfaction to be obtained from dwelling in the silent regions, but is it truly human life to do this exclusively? Meditation is dangerous. It can ruin a person's capacity for ordinary life if the states of calmness and meaningfulness are not translated into action. From the power behind the silence arises the possibility of creativity. Any action, however banal, can be transformed into a creative act. Otherwise, the energy gained from meditation, which must go into something, will almost inevitably be taken into the ego, strengthening a sense of one's own spirituality or power.

Meditation is not an end in itself. Whatever stage you have reached, there is always more, always further to go. However, it is not an infinite journey in the sense of moving ever further away from where you started, with no sense of arriving anywhere that you can call home. It is more like a series of arrivals, of breaking through to new areas of meaning where it is tempting to settle for what has been gained and aspire no further. Achievements in meditation are traps for the unwary or those who try to go it alone from the beginning.

One of the most important break-throughs is the realization that you have not moved somewhere else, or become someone else. You have not, if you see clearly and honestly enough, turned into some rarefied, holy being, inhabiting remote regions of elevated consciousness – a possibility which most of us have initially as a mental image of where meditation might lead. You discover that you are still exactly yourself, and it comes as a revelation, because although you are none other than yourself, that self has undergone transformations, and is a great deal more powerful. The transformations are subtle, because they are not external, and where there are external changes – the wearing of special clothes or of a special expression, ostentatious changes of life-style, the embracing of a set of special 'wholesome' or 'holy' habits – beware! Real internal transformation does not need these props.

It is a serious and potent revelation, occurring about at the stage with which this chapter has been concerned, to realize that *you*, not some elevated and future version of yourself, are now a person with responsibilities of a kind which once you would not have believed yourself capable of meeting. You know now that you are, but it still takes an effort to claim this knowledge, and not to fall back into operating from your old self-image, with its familiar and practised set of responses and reactions. You come to see yourself exactly as you are, but what you are is more than what you thought once upon a time.

Chapter 11

Contemplation

This chapter is dealing with an advanced stage of meditation. If parts of the chapter seem obscure, it is because contemplative states are difficult to convey in imagery, and the theory will not be very meaningful until it becomes personally important, the result of meditating for many years.

Progress in meditation does not mean acquiring the ability to sit motionless in meditation for hours if not years. It is essential to distinguish between the *practice* of meditation as an activity which is separate from the rest of life and the *state* of meditation which is not limited to designated sessions, nor dependent on stillness, silence, or concentration on a technique. The method is only a training in establishing the state. The training is indispensable, however. There is no short-cut to acquiring knowledge of meditation and the ability to hold meditative awareness so that you can act from the place of meditation within you, whatever you are doing. It is the same as with playing the piano: the state in which glorious music will flow effortlessly from your finger-tips is the result of long hours of practice, training your fingers to respond automatically, increasing your ability to comprehend musical notation, developing your understanding of music and musicality. The end result is that the production of music on a piano becomes second nature, provided you keep in practice.

Similarly, with meditation training, the state can become natural. Eventually, washing-up, programming computers, arguing, sex, can all be meditative, performed with the essence of meditation uninterrupted. Your attention is on the task in hand, but there is another dimension to it. This is the objective of all the hours spent practising the technique. You may only be able to achieve this state for moments, but the relationship between meditation and living should become more and more inextricable. It is the heart of the challenge which meditation offers.

The Conscious Imperative

Sooner or later it becomes evident to a meditator how desirable it would be if the level of consciousness, and all that goes with it in a meditation session, could be continued and extended into daily life. During a session your conscious activity is a simple state of bare observation without the usual internal interference. Sometimes, for a while afterwards, you are able to keep awareness in every action and perception. Then your awareness is caught by the complexities of life, and there are only the complexities. You are no longer conscious of yourself and them equally. Because your consciousness is caught up in them, you become identified with cooking a meal, wrestling with the economics of your business, serving the deluge of demands your children generate, and You, the consciousness of yourself as the doer, go missing. Next time you sit down to meditate, you find yourself again, and there can be such refreshment in that finding, such a sense of wholeness, clarity or peace that the intervening time seems like a wild hurly-burly of lost consciousness, and you wonder how you could have allowed yourself to descend into it and lose an awareness so precious and simplifying. And so it goes on, losing and finding, losing and finding.

Consciousness is a twenty-four hour activity. Maintaining the level of conscious awareness which is achieved through meditation becomes more and more possible with time, will and effort. The desire to hold on to a wider awareness could be called the conscious imperative, because the more you know of what consciousness can be, the more undesirable it seems to act mechanically, reacting in a habitual manner without proper self-awareness.

When the state of meditation becomes a reality for you, when what was theory becomes personal experience, then you will know the difference between meditation and the techniques of meditation. A technique is a guide through subtle and gross levels of mind. Without such a guide you become lost. When you let go of the technique during a meditation session you revert to daydreaming, or literally fall asleep, or pursue some pocket of consciousness to the exclusion of others because it seems terribly meaningful and you feel it must be of profound meditational importance. In other words, you become identified. This can happen at any level.

You cannot do without the training of the technique, but when you know meditation itself, it is like uncovering a part of you which has always been there, but of which you have just not been particularly aware before. Permanent awareness of it is the result of many, many hours of conscious work during and outside formal sessions, but it is within reach of all of us. It is awareness of your own being. Whether you recollect it at any moment or not is irrelevant to the fact that it is always there. Eventually, you do not have to sit quietly to know it; you can go to it at any time, as if to a temple within, and life looks different, and is different. Choices can be made from this point in you, and from it you can act rather than react in situations. It is not that you necessarily see things like this *all* the time; rather, it is that you can turn your mind to it whenever you want to.

Once perceived in yourself in a more or less permanent way, it becomes possible and important to see it in others, in other people, in all forms of life, even in inanimate objects. You begin to see why people act the way they do. Morality takes on a new meaning, and compassion and understanding arise. True compassion originates not from sentimentality, but from seeing clearly.

Contemplation

The ability to hold self-awareness is the prerequisite for contemplation. Meditation employs technique, but when contemplation is possible, techniques are no longer necessary in the same way. Contemplation could be likened to a simple gazing. There are stages of contemplation. It may be you gazing, or there may be just gazing. Consciousness may be attached to an identity, or resting in itself. Then your individual identity is no different from that of anyone else. It becomes not so much my essence, as essence in me.

Through contemplation you, the individual, are in contact with the macrocosm. The perennial question, 'Is the Divine outside or inside, transcendent or immanent?' no longer needs to be asked. The answer is evidently 'both' – but 'inside' and 'outside' are no longer what you thought. There is not much point in trying to describe it; you become bogged down in grand-sounding concepts like 'cosmic consciousness' and 'All is One', which mean nothing in the absence of personal experience, and can actually stand in the way of it.

Contemplation is a stage after the fulfilment of your natural motivation. The thrust and direction provided by your personal need decree what you will find and how you will see 'reality'. When this impulse is no longer a determining factor, pushing you onward, you either stop, or your will needs to come into operation. To go further, you must perfect the capacity to look upon all things great and small with an equal gaze, seeing them for what they are, perceiving the essence of them, and knowing that they are all contained within a unity which is more than the sum total of all the individual essences.

There is almost a vacuum left where natural motivation once carried you forward, and it takes will to fill it, will to cross the expanse between the known and the unknown, and to turn the gaze of contemplation upon this or upon that, when there is no particular personal need to do it. Contemplation is being able to gaze without limitation, without the boundaries of labels, from a position of equanimity.

How Meditation Prepares the Psyche

It is meditation which makes contemplation possible (other than momentarily), because otherwise you do not have the internal structure to sustain the contemplative perspective, unlocalized and undivided as it is. Properly, meditation is a training in the realization that there is always *more*, and it gradually builds up familiarity with a previously unknown psychological terrain, establishing the appropriate internal organization so that power-ful experiences are not destructive. Without a psychological structure which can integrate these meaningfully, personal equilibrium can be upset. The result can be various states of delusion, megalomania or religious fanaticism; or, in some cases, the fear of what might come through keeps the doors to higher perceptions firmly banged shut.

One of the indications of an unprepared psyche is when extended perception is accompanied by an enormous emotional charge. Over the course of years, a meditator will encounter as natural results of meditation, experiences which, in isolation or when triggered 'accidentally', might have seemed vastly important. Meditation introduces most categories of deeper human experience, but only when the meditator is in a position to cope with them. All the while it is building a conceptual and emotional framework based on graduated experience, and within the security and demands of the discipline, so that increased energy, powerful insights and changes in perspective or values are received quietly and integrated; valued, but treated as 'no big deal'.

Some esoteric traditions speak of a guardian or sentinel before the portals of 'higher knowledge', preventing the unworthy or uninitiated from entering, lest they be blasted. It is an apt description of the process. The guardian is that part of an individual which preserves personal integrity, in the sense of a functioning psychological entity. In the face of anything which might threaten the stability of that 'self', there is an instinctive fear, or rejection. The guardian is doing its job. However, the sentinel is also there to be passed. Access cannot be denied to anyone with the right credentials – which is another way of saying that anyone with the psychological organization to be able to integrate radical changes of perspective, inevitably affecting his or her sense of self, without becoming unhinged, is able to proceed. For these the guardian has no terrors.

Beyond the Conscious Threshold

Through meditation you may reach knowledge of God in the form which is most meaningful for you. The star, the void, and communion are beyond theology; they represent direct knowledge. But the journey is not concluded. It stretches beyond the threshold of consciousness, beyond your individual identity, and anything you may claim for yourself. The journey is infinite, as is the divine creativity which perpetually maintains existence.

The voyager, for whom meditation has been the means of reaching the point of being able to gaze upon the three faces of the divine in creation, must progress to a realization of the unity which encompasses all aspects and for which no images are adequate. This progression can be symbolized by leaving the boat behind. Where technique is concerned, it involves moving from reliance on the familiar procedures of meditation into the subtle relationship of contemplation. Inevitably there will be attachment to meditation, a tendency to lean on the method which has been entirely adequate so far, and has provided security and meaning. However, there is no method as such in the unknown, except the 'knack' of contemplation, how to gaze upon what is, or how simply to gaze. Once you know what this 'gazing' is, it requires no method to get to it, but is instantaneous. The purpose of the method is to get to the place where contemplation becomes possible.

Contemplation can be like embracing a strange nothingness, for which everything, even personal identity, must be left behind. Or it may seem to be embracing immensity or eternity, with a sense of great potency hidden in the darkness. Either way, fear is the last barrier to be conquered. You must give up your gods and everything with meaning; there is no greater nakedness. It is sometimes called dying to yourself. The transition from meditation to contemplation requires sobriety and faith, and the moving force is your will, because emotional motivations have no meaning when personal fulfilment is not the aim.

It is not difficult to find references to this stage in the appropriate literature. It is usually associated with images of darkness, or void, because you are entering an unknown dimension, following an instinct at some primary level of being which cannot be known in the usual ways. It is dark, too, because there are no reference points, and no map to follow. You are opening your awareness to an area which is beyond the threshold of consciousness. The tools of normal consciousness cannot define, label or classify what is encountered here, nor can it be 'brought back' and added to the furniture of the conscious mind.

It can only be known, and the knowledge will work in its own way.

When your whole being is gathered into the realization, contemplation is a jump. The image of a leap into the dark is a familiar one, even used colloquially. Anyone can imagine what it might feel like to leap blind, as off a cliff, into the unknown. You would need a great deal of trust, in the creative potential of the leap, in your own resources, and in the necessity for the leap. The only thing which could over-rule all your instincts for self-preservation and your extreme fear would be your will. Will is developed by the discipline of meditation, and in the internal leap it is all you have to enable you to enter the darkness of contemplation as a foundation for your life.

We have equated meditation with a boat, a vehicle to travel through a terrain which cannot be crossed without a suitable vessel. Material ships traverse expanses of water or space. In the meditative analogy it is the ocean of being which is crossed, through complexities of experience to pure contemplation of the source. The image of 'leaping' out of the boat is experientially accurate. It describes the quality of the realization, and the sort of letting go which is required. In addition, there is a further refinement of the image which some may find useful. Men and women handle the inner journey differently. The stages are the same, the method of meditation is equally valid, and realization is of the same order, but at the root of individual differences in the way experience is encountered there is the essential male and the essential female impulse.

The profound experience of letting go of what you have held on to longest, your sense of personal identity, may reveal a primary differentiation in approach. For men, the stage of leaving the boat behind is akin to a jump, an exercise of will to project themselves into the void, away from the last support. For women, on the other hand, it is more like discovering that the boat *is* no support, and is no longer necessary. It is still possible to cling to it, just as no one can push you into leaping before you decide to act of your own will. However, the woman who enthrones herself in the darkness has overcome fear. The darkness of experience to which a human being opens him or herself in surrendering self-interest contains sheer power. Women embody power; men wield it.

Power and Creativity

Creative power needs a vehicle for it to manifest itself. When an individual becomes aware of this possibility through the eye of contemplation, there is an obligation to use this power. Every action of life must be a creative action, not a reaction, and this means maintaining a level of conscious awareness in whatever you do. Each day is composed of action. In the end, what does it matter what people think, or even feel? It is what they *do* which has a bearing on others. It is 'doing' which creates the pattern of a life, setting up conditions for events to arise. You may really feel a great deal of affection for the family cat, but if you kick it out of the way whenever you are in a temper, what is poor pussy to think? You may have a great desire to see peace in the world, and talk a great deal about it, but if your home front is an emotional battleground, or you are determined to fight for what you see as your personal 'rights', what are you actually doing to bring about peace in the world which surrounds you?

Conscious action needs no special scenario. It does not operate with a fanfare, nor does the capacity to act creatively elevate the doer into a being with godlike status. The power dwells in silence and darkness. When it manifests itself it retains these characteristics. Real power is revealed through action, but it does not necessarily draw attention to itself. The appearance may be no more notable than a well-integrated life lived by a person of stature, who is able to act with courage and clarity and call upon a great deal of strength and power when they are needed.

Creativity speaks for itself. What is more, it exists for itself and works for its own ends, not for the glorification of the person who acts as a channel. However, human beings are not merely passive vehicles, separate from and not entirely responsible for the workings of some greater force. They are conscious, and the responsibilities of consciousness have been dealt with at length. Human beings command and embody a creative power – as individuals. The notion of collective responsibility is usually an excuse; only through the will of individuals is any achievement brought about. The obligation to create through a conscious life is service to the world, and it represents divine creativity expressing itself through human beings. Many traditional teachings speak of the countless names of God: the many aspects of divinity. Creativity is one such name for the ultimate source, for the godhead. It describes the aspect of power in manifestation, which can only operate in the physical sphere through a physical operator.

Human beings are creators: wielders of creative consciousness. Animals are conscious, but they do not create consciously. Human beings have the potential for doing so, whether or not they are aware of it. Every person creates his or her own life, in every detail. This is a very difficult realization. It is easier to blame external circumstances, society, other people's inadequacies, fate, luck; anything but oneself, especially if an event seems to come out of the blue with no obvious direct connection with anything one has done to 'cause' it.

Causality is very complex, and its logic is not necessarily visible. There are many levels of causality. It works within the unconscious and with constellations of meaning, not with single factors which can be readily identified. It may stretch a long way back in time, or take on most meaning in connection with the future. What is more, it is easy to be superstitious about causes. When an unexpected misfortune strikes, there is a tendency to wonder: What have I done to deserve this? What am I being punished for? In the overall causality of your personal life and actions, misfortune has meaning, but it is not as simplistic as crime and punishment. What is significant is how you react to the misfortune, because this will condition your future.

Unlike all other species on this earth, human beings can reflect upon themselves, and can be aware of consciousness itself. We can be aware of the source of the creative power which brings about the result of our choices and actions. The way to bring an end to suffering is by acknowledging and taking responsibility for the power we have.

The Power of Choice

We humans are born with a stupendous power, which we cannot but use, the power of choice. Even a baby has it, right from the beginning: the choice to cry or not to cry, and at what pitch.

Limited in scope the exercise of this infantile choice may be, but not in power, as every parent knows. The power of an infant to influence life and people around it is awe-inspiring.

It is worth looking more closely at this primary choice-making, because it illustrates in a simple form principles which are exactly the same when life is a great deal more complex. A baby is not an automaton, driven by uncontrollable sensations with automatic consequences such as tears. There may, for example, be hunger sensations in the stomach. Baby has a number of options: to wake and scream, to wake and cry, to wake and lie making sounds indicative of discomfort, to wake and ignore the specific sensations of hunger because he or she trusts the situation, or finds something else external or internal of more interest. It is entirely up to the young human being how he or she chooses to deal with the situation, at least initially. (A baby's instinct to cry in order to draw attention to its needs is also a primary survival mechanism which will eventually take over if the needs remain unsatisfied.) However, that there is a range of options and the power to choose action is often unrecognized by adults who assume that a baby cannot help his reactions, possibly because they assume the same about themselves. Conscious beings have choice, and babies are conscious.

Of the possible courses of action in this illustration, the screaming option requires the least effort and consciousness. It is immediate, requires no thought, and would seem to promise the quickest results. However, though results may be quicker, they are also more likely to create a tired, anxious, bad-tempered food-source, an inadequate supply, an incapacity to digest it properly, less time therefore to interact happily with the environment, less time to be *conscious* of surroundings, and so on, in an escalating chain of consequences. Likewise, the other options will create other situations. A combination of the baby's own choice and the mother's choice of response will increasingly, in this early example, condition the way baby chooses, although it can never remove from him the power or ability to choose.

The more an individual's power of choice is acknowledged and respected, the greater the possibilities for consciousness. Every choice, every reaction and feeling for which responsibility is taken, as opposed to attributing them to forces over which you have no control, returns you to the creative source within. Actions which consciously originate from this source create a different set of consequences from those which arise unconsciously. It is impossible not to create your life; the choice is to do it creatively.

Endings and Beginnings

No longer dependent on a boat, having exercised your will for the greatest act of courage so far required, where do you find yourself after surrendering so much to the unknown? Not only back in the place of setting out, but realizing that the sensation of leaving it behind was an illusion. Ordinary life is still ordinary life. The obligations are still there, the irritations are still there, the pleasures are still there. However, you are no longer identified with them, or dependent upon them for your well-being and sense of identity. And you have a new set of obligations arising from the realm to which you now possess the key.

Contemplation is possible at any time, in any place. It is not that the boat of meditation has been abandoned; it is still available, still useful. Meditation can be used to establish the conditions for contemplation when the perspective is lost, or to re-establish calmness, or to raise energy, or to locate the place of meditation in order to act from it, or simply for meditation's sake.

The journey proves to be circular, or rather spiral. There is a progression, if it is pursued long enough, but you do not find yourself somewhere else entirely. The old analogy of needing to reach the summit of the mountain and then return again is saying the same thing. Remaining at the top is not useful to others, or to the Creator whose manifestation is creation, or to yourself, except as a retreat.

Yet the journey is not an illusion. It feels exactly as if you are setting out on a journey when you take up an activity which requires reorganization of your life and self-discipline, and which leads you to discover constantly new perspectives and meanings. Sometimes it seems that you have moved a very long way from where you started. Your values are different, your fundamental outlook may have changed, your preoccupations, life-style and relationships may have altered, and there are periods when you feel very alone. Such is the nature of human development, that there is suffering, but also, as one great meditator has pointed out, an end to suffering.

When you discover that, despite having changed so much internally and died to your old self, you are very much alive, still part of the familiar world, still with friends, still anchored by the necessity to earn a living or look after a family, it is an introduction to real joy. Joy of this kind is very stable. It cannot be taken away because it is not dependent on external conditions. It is not a feeling to be sought for its own sake and lost when clouds cover the sun. The sun, the creative maintainer of life, the power source, is now internal. Knowledge of joy brings with it knowledge of sorrow, but such sorrow is a long way from preoccupation with personal suffering. It gives true understanding and compassion.

One weakness in the image of a journey is the suggestion of a linear progression. The stages of meditation are distinct, and in the long term successive, but they do not emerge neatly one after the other. In every phase there are intimations and experiences of different degrees of meditation. The grand challenges are met continually in circumstances which may not appear very momentous externally, but which require considerable conscious effort to act on the principle involved. Every time, there is a chance to make a jump. You do not leap once only, but many times, each demanding the exercise of will, courage and conscious choice. At a certain stage, the leap becomes a total change of consciousness, but this degree is only possible because the principle is familiar.

The development of consciousness is not like climbing a ladder, so that you can only operate from the rung on which your being is currently situated. The full scope and the timeless dimension are present in every moment. At different times you gain some experience of all aspects of the totality, even though your being may not be able to maintain the realization for long. You cannot save up your energy and will for the big challenges by ignoring the seemingly little. Strength is cumulative. Every instance of lack of courage or self-indulgence sets you back a little, no matter how apparently minor the issue, and every act of strength and consciousness will increase your conscious foundation and make further such actions easier.

Creativity is not a current which is only switched on after a certain point. It is available right from the beginning. It enters with consciousness, and creativity is in every moment as full and as true to itself as your conscious actions will allow. The temple within is always present; you train yourself to be aware of it.

The Gates of Life and Death

Meditation brings a knowledge of life, and also of death. The phrase 'dying to yourself' is not a metaphor. When the clinging to all the things which previously represented identity and meaning has been left behind, and is replaced by a knowledge of immensity, eternity and change within your being, then physical dying is no longer a terror, no longer an ending, no longer unknown. Through meditation you learn the nature of death, and experience it. It is neither an ending, nor truly a beginning, for these are temporal concepts. Rather death is present within life, can be known at every moment for what it is, and fear drops away.

There is no better preparation for physical death. Some traditions have emphasized this aspect, and Books of the Dead are both meditation manuals and preparation for dying. The descriptions by those who have clinically died, and returned, may sound familiar to someone with meditation experience. They often speak of a great peace, space, light, or a figure of light, and there is frequently a sense of reluctance to lose awareness of these by returning to the limitations of the body. For those who do, it is because of a sense that it is not yet time to leave the physical. There are other kinds of experience too; there are those who encounter the reality known as hell.

None of these descriptions *are* the reality; they reflect the individual's state of being at the time of physical death, and what he or she knows as life. Hence the importance of preparation, and of the attitude with which an individual meets death. Consciousness transcends the apparent boundaries between states of life and death. It is possible to stand in full consciousness before the gates of life and death, gazing upon them as upon any other object of contemplation. The gates of life and death are within every human being. We cannot avoid knowing them at some point, but with conscious awareness the knowledge can be a foundation for living, not a summary and conclusion. It could be said that at every moment we are making choices which will determine the time and manner of our death. The more we are aware of this power, the more important every action becomes, that consciousness be increased not diminished.

Chapter 12

Unity

Evolution and Consciousness

Meditation is as old as the human race. From the most ancient civilization we have evidence of the inner journey in the form of mythology, much of which is describing in image and narrative the type of experience for which no other enduring material record is possible. Objects have also come down to us, testifying to a universal preoccupation with a sacred dimension of life and its expression in symbolic form. There are figures, pictures, ritual artifacts, and the testimony of standing stones, speaking across millennia in a language which is as current today as it was then, although so seldom understood. It is through meditation that the language of sacred symbolism becomes more comprehensible.

Evolution as it affects humankind is the evolution of consciousness. It leaves no traces as such, except the world as a whole. Compare the scope of today's consciousness, which includes an awareness of sub-molecular particles, of the possibilities of altering the DNA code, of the nuclear processes within stars, and of the structure of galaxies, to that which, for example, had just comprehended how to keep records by chiselling stone tablets, how to move about slowly in wheeled vehicles, or knew the greater universe only through studying patterns and movements of tiny points of light in the heavens. The difference is not so much in the quantity of information as in the level of conceptual ability human beings command to extract information from the world about. The information available to anyone living today is different from that available four thousand years ago, in the degree of abstraction upon which it is based. Our current understanding of the nature of creation demands a bigger perspective. What we know as ordinary reality constitutes our consciousness. This ordinary reality has increased vastly in complexity, and to this extent at least, consciousness is on a wider foundation.

The nature of consciousness, as has been suggested, is simple; but the wider the awareness of complexity, the deeper the simplicity which can be apprehended from it. For example, if simplicity is characterized by *economy* as a principle, there are ways of increasing simplicity in some areas of life, which open new possibilities in others. It is far more economical of time and energy to drive four hundred miles than to walk it on foot, or to travel by oxen-cart. It is even more economical of human resources to fly the distance. Again, if the object is to communicate with people a long way away, it is more economical still to speak to them from where you are, by telephone or satellite link. The time and energy saved can be used for a multitude of other purposes. It is not possible to design space-probes if all the faculties which make the conception possible are non-existent. Technology represents increasing simplification and greater economy of means, and from it has resulted an enormous extension of possibilities.

Everyday reality is of a different order now from what it has been in the past, and that is a mark of a change in the general level of consciousness. If you were to equate consciousness with elevated states which transcend the everyday and bear little relationship to it, or with interest in areas classified as mystical, you might be tempted to think that the level of consciousness nowadays is not very high, or has even regressed from a golden age. But the greater majority of people are as they have always been, preoccupied to a greater or lesser extent with material things, with personal benefit, with the drive towards recognition and status, and with making war on those who pursue these things differently. Some people have always sought and found a wider reality. To do this they have had to re-evaluate their own preoccupations and train their awareness and perception through self-discipline. Although the general consciousness of a time and culture is the level from which you start, individual growth in consciousness is not dependent upon it. The continued existence of war, strife, greed and mismanagement in human society is not the standard by which the level of consciousness can be judged. Nor is a simple society, in which these negative elements appear to be minimal, necessarily exemplifying a high level of consciousness.

It is a question of scale. Global culture represents a larger scale of society than has existed before in human history. The negative elements are more obvious and more potent in their ramifications and therefore more alarming, but at the same time the creative possibilities are much greater. Anyway, the process of evolution is irreversible. If you take into consideration both ends of the spectrum, the best and the worst, perhaps the balance has not changed very much. Only the scale has, but this in itself implies that the mean level of consciousness may well have increased.

Meditation is a major tool in the evolution of consciousness, and always has been. The urge to meditate has somewhere in its roots the question: What is the life of a man or woman if, like a mayfly, it exists only to reproduce itself, and pass into the great on-going wheel of the species? Where is the wheel going? Is a human life really equivalent in its characteristics to that of a coral animal, serving a purpose of no greater scope than this?

Human instincts are categorical in their reply; an individual's sense of self is, by its existence, a refutation of the comparison. Mayflys and Anthozoa do not have such a sense of self, nor the instinct to want to know why they live as they do, or what purpose their species may serve in a larger order. Human beings who take up an activity like meditation are responding to a drive within their species-nature to utilize more of themselves, and this utilization increases the sum of consciousness within the species and in the world.

Only individuals can bring it about. One of the most meaningful reasons for meditation is that increasing consciousness in yourself also increases it in the world. The sum total on the planet at any one time is greater, through the action of one individual on it. And increasing consciousness is not directly analogous to casting a vote in a national election, or adding a drop to the sea. The incremental effects work on a different principle. Consciousness is not molecular or granular, a matter of individual units which add together one by one to make a grand total. It is a unity, every part affecting every other. It undergoes and initiates non-quantifiable transformations, and it is a potent force in itself.

The inter-connectedness of consciousness and the effect of one individual upon the totality are often misunderstood by an idea that it is the action of meditating which 'raises' the consciousness of the world. It is not the meditation sessions, but the integrity of the intervening periods, how a person handles the crises of personal life, which constitute increased consciousness in action. This is the way in which meditation trains and enables consciousness to be 'raised'.

The Lineage of Meditation

Meditation must be seen from a larger perspective. It has existed from the beginning of humanity, and will do so into the future, and those who make it part of their life enter into a long line or communion of those who have valued and practised it.

Any major human activity can be viewed as a lineage. The tradesman of today is faced with the same type of problems, and will have to make the same type of decisions as his forebear three thousand years ago in an Egyptian city. The details differ, but in essence the principles of arranging capital, cashflow, profit margin, what to buy, and where to sell belong to the nature of trading. Likewise, the warriors/fighters of every age encounter the same situations, submit themselves to the same type of discipline; know the boredom, the risks, the exhilaration of combat; face death and the loss of comrades; and discover the fraternity of a shared commitment. Weaponry changes, but the psychology of it, the emotional values and moral confrontations before every individual soldier make him part of a human community which transcends time and stretches into the remote past. Every agriculturalist is subject to the vagaries of the environment and climate; every pastoralist and keeper of animals knows the terror of disease, the management of pasture and fodder, and so on. Women in childbirth become aware of being part of a sisterhood, ancient and current, of all the countless women who have undergone the same trial of pain and joy.

The more emotion is involved, the more meaningful is the recognition of lineage, and the more it is evoked as a source of strength. The history of his regiment is kept alive for a soldier, because it is a constant reminder that he is part of a larger whole, and this acts both as a counter to personal aggrandizement and as a source of pride and strength. Many a soldier has discovered courage in himself he did not know he had, not because his own life was in danger, but for the sake of the regiment, and more abstractly still, to uphold the role of Soldiering which he has chosen.

In a similar way, women as mothers can draw on a collective strength in times of difficulty or grief. Every mother watching by the bedside of a sick child knows how many other mothers have felt the same as she, and in the dark, silent hours of the night, the awareness can become very alive, with a sense of strength or 'tallness' almost palpably flowing into her from that vast sisterhood.

The lineage of meditation is a powerful reality. Every meditator becomes consciously a part, firstly, of the lineage of his particular system, and secondly, of the lineage of meditation itself, which is even longer and more potent than any individual line, because it links into the essence of meditation. This book has been written from within, and to evoke this lineage.

Meditation in Perspective

There is a need for meditation in the world, as there is a need for tradesmen, doctors, teachers, soldiers, mothers, fathers and so on. These are, or can be, roles of service. Whether they *are* depends entirely on how the participators view their roles. The attitude can be one of getting what you can out of it for yourself, or of serving others, or of upholding an ancient and honourable profession. Even jobs like removing rubbish or sweeping the streets can be viewed in these three ways. They need to be done, and they are tasks both ancient and entirely honourable if the doer sees them as such, and he or she acquires dignity thereby. Much unhappiness springs from the tyranny of the first viewpoint. It is ultimately an enslavement: slavery which is self-imposed.

Meditation also has a foundation in one of three overall

intentions, although these are not so much a question of personal attitude as a natural part of the process. They represent stages of growth in the understanding of meditation and indicate the centre of gravity which characterizes each stage. A meditator progresses through the three lines of meditation, which may be summarized as:

1. Meditation for yourself
2. Meditation for the world/others/tradition/humankind
3. Meditation for meditation's sake

The first line of meditation is where everyone starts. The others may be present in intention to some degree, but the first stage of meditation is concerned with training the meditator, and with developing the skills and capacities of being which will enable the other lines to be effective. Initially, meditating for yourself is entirely valid, in the sense of work upon an individual being, and personal benefits follow from it. It becomes a limitation, however, if the benefits are regarded as ends in themselves, or if the other lines do not develop along with meditation. The first line is an essential prerequisite.

This book has been primarily about the first line of meditation. The metaphor of a journey is a description of personal growth, of how meditation affects you, the individual.

The second line represents a change of emphasis, away from oneself as an individual, and towards a larger goal. It arises properly when something of the power and scope of meditation become a reality, and when meditation is well-established. It is built on the foundation of the first line, and is characterized by the perspective of meditation as a service for the benefit of others.

It is a distinct shift when the 'thirst' which had originally propelled a person into serious meditation dies away, and there is no particular personal reason to continue pushing forward. Reasons there are, but they are no longer so personal. For example, one of the ways of serving others or the world is to teach meditation, to repay one's debt to the system or tradition by taking on the responsibilities of teaching others. There is an obligation to perpetuate the teaching, which does not mean that everyone has to teach techniques as such. However, debts have to be repaid in some way or other.

The principle that increasing consciousness in oneself will increase it in the world is also to do with the second line. Again, this can be seen as an obligation.

There are meditational practices in some traditions which are designed to introduce the element of meditating for humanity. However, when meditation is still based in the first line, as a discipline of personal training, it may be stressed that the purpose of such practices is to develop an outwardly-directed capacity in the heart of the meditator, not to 'do anything' in the world. This is quite correct. The concept of 'meditating for humanity' lends itself to sentimental and fanciful notions, and may become a substitute for the effort of self-discipline. It is not possible to do for others what you are not able to do within yourself. However, the intention of meditating for humanity prepares the way for a shift in one's centre of gravity.

Meditation for the world is one of the justifications for enclosed or monastic life. This book has stressed that meditation belongs in the heart of life, no matter what the situation, and that it is not necessary to design ideal conditions to pursue it. This is in order to counter the idea that conditions specifically geared to assisting meditation are better – especially if the motivation behind such a move is the negative one of retreat. However, specialized centres of contemplative life, of groups of men and women dedicated to prayer and meditation, have their place, and very much serve a purpose in the world. They act as pointers, as reminders, and they generate a particular type of conscious energy within the body of humanity. Within the ethos of contemplative orders the idea of service is fundamental. Three lines are present in religious life when individuals undertake personal work and discipline, consciously dedicated to the service of humanity, and for the glory or service of God.

Where there is consciousness there is power, and where there is power there will be effects. However, the effects will be neither direct nor measurable, and it is never possible to know all the consequences of any action, much less concerning a reality as large and complex as humanity. Therefore it is wise to be circumspect about meditating with an intention of bringing about any specific effect in the world, as an end in itself. In a wider perspective, what is good for humanity as a whole may be very different from what individuals imagine it to be, and such intentions may stand in the way of developing the third line of meditation.

For there is a further shift possible, which is meditation for the sake of meditation. This is the stage of going beyond one's particular tradition, and working to perpetuate meditation in itself. It is a perpetuation of the knowledge of meditation.

It is important to bear in mind the difference between techniques of meditation and the essence of it. The essence of meditation remains constant, as do the principles by which it works. However, times change, and people and cultures change. Approaches to meditation, the form the techniques take, the theoretical base of it and the mythology – all these need reformulation from time to time to take account of change in the world. All the classic texts on meditation were particularly appropriate when they arose, for the people of that time, in their cultural situation. By and large, they are classics because they were themselves reformulations by someone who understood the process and could express it in a way which was appropriate, and needed at the time. If they are considered classic, it is also because they transcend their time, and are still worth reading for the insight into meditation which they contain. Other books may be 'of interest', but the ones which are formative and widely enduring are not just expositions of their tradition, but shed light on meditation itself. The essence of meditation needs to be apprehended anew before the approach to it can be reformulated or developed.

Understanding the essence is arrived at by knowing a particular system and recognizing its worth, but also by knowing that which transcends it. Reformulations tend to occur when there is a need, because the conditions of the time have changed and a new form for the teaching and promoting of meditation is demanded. An example of this occurred within Buddhism when it was imported into Japan, via China, from its origins in India. In the conditions of a very different culture, an entirely new form arose: Zen, which took the emphasis away from theory and introduced the koan (a paradoxical statement or question) as a meditation device. It is not known exactly how this came about, but the culture which produced samurai also produced this approach to meditation.

Reformulation has continually taken place within a living discipline like meditation, it will continue to do so into the future, and is undoubtedly taking place now in response to the needs of the time, which have altered radically. For a start, a new culture has come into being, a global culture with a new foundation, both territorial and psychological. Previous national cultures still exist, as previous meditation traditions still exist, and for many they are adequate. However, across the boundaries between these there is a culture for which former moral codes and beliefs have become invalidated by change, and an increasingly huge number of people live within this culture and give it their primary allegiance. The rise of a world society represents a change of perspective, and it introduces new needs.

The parameters of world-culture are defined by telecommunications possibilities, its frontiers by the ocean of Space, and its power by nuclear, biogenetic and computer capabilities. The birth of this pan-earth society is accompanied by the sort of fragmentation which has its parallel whenever a small-scale society has encountered and been succeeded by a larger-scale, more advanced one. There is a breakdown of moral and religious values, disorientation and excesses, resistance to the ineluctable march of still barely understood processes, and a tremendous fear of the future. When old-established values and ways of doing things become less certain or out-moded, the future seems more unknown, unpredictable and alien than ever before. The transition is painful until social, moral and sacred values are established, following those of the dominant culture, or, in the current situation, until they can be *created* to hold the new together, and give it a stable psychological foundation.

Creating such values is a matter of consciousness, of including changed situation, a changed world, into the consciousness of human beings. The need to work on consciousness is constant, and takes on urgency in times of crisis. Indeed, crisis can be viewed as a means of *forcing* growth in consciousness. The reformulation of meditation in line with the needs of the time *will* take place, because it is a response to an imperative within the nature of Homo Sapiens to perpetuate consciousness; to perpetuate what is unique to the species. Consciousness is perpetuated by re-forming as needed. The perpetuation of the existing forms is not perpetuation of consciousness; the former is an obligation of the second line of meditation, the latter belongs to the third line.

Much of the confusion in the picture which is presented of meditation, now that it has come into the market-place, results from a lack of perspective. Under the heading 'Meditation' are both techniques for alleviating gastric complaints and promises of a passport to cosmic consciousness, with all varieties in between.

The three lines of meditation, that is, the scope which it has from the least to the most, are part of a unity, and they all need to be acknowledged. If they are not, meditation becomes devalued, either a commodity which is too cheap, or a wayward minority interest. Meditating for oneself, for whatever reason, holds open possibilities if its function in the world and a sense of its scope are also present, even embryonically, in the awareness of the meditator. If he or she should wish to go further, the door is open to the full realization of the three lines.

Meditation and the Future

The urge to proliferate human life, on this planet and any other which can be reached, has the imperative of growth in consciousness at its heart, because human life is conscious life. Other species also proliferate, until they are checked by limited territory or predators. But what if the nature of self-aware consciousness, and all the skills and adaptability which go with it, make available almost unlimited territory (at least compared with what we know so far on little Earth), and therefore unlimited resources, so that the population is never forced to stabilize in numbers to survive within a limited environment, and in addition there is no outside predator? Where does it end? How far, in all senses, can we go, and why?

It is worthwhile to ask these questions, not to receive ultimate answers, but because questions epitomize the out-reaching aspect of consciousness. Questions generate more questions, constantly directing energy into the quest for conscious knowledge. Once you accept an answer as final, the process stops.

The average ancient, medieval, or even nineteenth-century

man could look ahead to the future and expect to see it as similar to the present, perhaps with a few refinements representing progress. Not so any more. The cumulative effects of accelerating change make the future seem awesome, and for many who base their expectations of the future on the negative elements of the current transitional phase, potentially awful. However, all extrapolations are apt to leave out one key factor, the role of consciousness. It is a lack of courage and a failure of perspective to equate human nature with its worst manifestations. It is ignorance to underestimate the power of consciousness.

Because consciousness is inherently creative, it can bring about developments which are new, and entirely unforeseen. The seeds of the immediate future are present now, but it is impossible to be sure even in the short term exactly how they will develop. The general lines are reasonably obvious, following from a dramatic increase in power and the technology which goes with it. All power is dangerous, but it is also creative, and every manifestation of it is a consequence of human nature.

There is a school of thought which regards Nature, and what is 'natural', as rocks and soil, trees and vegetation, insects and animals, sea and sky. Human beings, in this view, are only being true to nature when living in close communion with these things, and utilizing products closely derived from them. However, from another perspective, it could be said that we are creators. It is our nature to create new and more efficient ways of doing things, and new materials, and human nature is as 'natural' as animal nature. A plastic cup is no more unnatural in principle than an earthenware bowl, a computer than an abacus, a nuclear energy generator than the sun, the energy source on which all life on earth is dependent for its very existence.

Whatever the human scenario in three thousand years, it will be our future, created by us, and not some alien progeny with which we can scarcely relate, and in which it is difficult to discover 'human' values. The greatest source of fear and uneasiness in face of the future is a limited view of what is human and of what our values are or could be. Values come from what is meaningful, and meaning arises from experience of deeper human needs than mere physical survival.

In other words, the role of work like meditation is crucial in putting meaning into the world we now inhabit and will inhabit. If human life still exists in three thousand years, the details and complexity of it are likely to be radically different from anything which we can conceive of now. However, two things will be constant in essence: human nature and consciousness. The essence of these can be known now as they will be then, and the aeons in between will be as nothing. From the simplicity of that knowledge, complexity is understandable, meaningful, and can be handled creatively and responsibly.

If, by then, our psychological centre is no longer the earth but the galaxy, it will be because we have developed not only the technology to exend into a wider realm of space, but the capacity to make it meaningful and to deal with whatever we may encounter. If we discover that we share a common galactic home with other beings, the detail of their environment, anatomy and psychology will be no barrier if they, too, are conscious beings. On that level we will meet as equals, able to know the same reality transcending our differences. They may have different gods, described in ways which reflect their nature, but the temple within will be the same. We, Homo Sapiens, will be compelled to know it as not a human temple only, but a galactic temple, and ultimately as a truly universal temple, founded in consciousness, and accessible to every conscious being within the universe.

Into that far future, the lineage of meditation will extend. Meditators then, as now, will be part of a common enterprise, and able to know the same essence within a still greater Unity. Meditation is a preparation for the future. The evolution of humanity and the survival of human consciousness do not depend on our turning into a race of super-humans, or on every person becoming somehow 'enlightened' with the result that wars, struggle and conflict cease. Rather our survival and evolution depend on the ability to cope with the demands and complexities of everyday reality, no matter how different from the past, whether on this planet or in space, and with whatever devices our inventiveness provides.

Both multitudinous complexity and the one essence of consciousness are within a Unity, which is visible as everything that exists in this universe – and in any others we may not yet know. All creation is within Unity.

SOME SUGGESTED READING

This list contains most of the classic meditation literature representing major traditions, and other works selected on the basis of their insight into the experience of meditation or stages in the growth of consciousness. Some are descriptive, some symbolic or allegorical, some analytic, and some in the form of aphorisms.

Where there is a standard or recommended edition, the details are listed, but many of these works exist in various translations. Some texts are interspersed with commentaries which purport to explain or expand the text. Such commentaries are best left unread; nothing more effectively destroys the power of the original than well-meaning elucidations.

Abulafia, Abraham: writings on Kabbalistic meditation
Attar, Farid Ud-Din: The Conference of the Birds
Avalon, Arthur (Sir John Woodroffe): The Serpent Power
Bhagavad Gita, The
Book of Jubilee, The: Cranswick Press, London, 1984
Buddhist Sutras and Suttas: many are directly relevant to meditation
Cloud of Unknowing, The
Dionysus the Areopagite: The Celestial Hierarchies
Herrigel, E.: Zen in the Art of Archery
Hilton, Walter: The Ladder (Scale) of Perfection
Ibn al-Arabi: works
I Ching
Kabbalah Unveiled, The: Transl. S.L. MacGregor Mathers, Routledge and Kegan Paul Ltd
Kempis, Thomas à: The Imitation of Christ
Lao Tsu: Tao Te Ching
Letters of the Scattered Brotherhood: Ed. Mary Strong, James Clarke and Co. Ltd, Cambridge
Meister Eckhart: Collected Works

Patanjali: Sutras

Philokalia

Secret of the Golden Flower, The: Transl. Richard Wilhelm, Routledge and Kegan Paul Ltd

Sefer Yetsirah (Book of Formation): early Kabbalah text

St John of the Cross: Collected Works

Suzuki, D.T.: author of many authoritative texts on Zen Buddhism

Ten Principal Upanishads: Ed. S. Purohit and W.B. Yeats, Faber

Tibetan Book of the Dead, The: Ed. W.Y. Evans Wentz, Oxford University Press

Visuddhi Magga (The Path of Purification): Bhadantacariya Buddhaghosa; a monumental and minutely detailed analysis of Theravada Buddhist meditation

Vivekachudamani (The Crest Jewel of Wisdom), Shri Shankaracharya: the least flowery versions of this great work are the most useful

Way of a Pilgrim, The: Transl. R.M. French

Wood, Ernest: Yoga, Pelican Pb

INDEX

160